What people are saying about *Intuitive Imagery* . . .

"The authors of this book are not merely hypothesizing about the importance of intuition, but describing the details of actual research and application using a powerful and repeatable intuitive methodology in real-life situations. These folks mean business, and they've proven that it's a resource that really works!" —**Henry Reed, Ph.D.**, professor of Transpersonal Studies, Atlantic University, author, *Exercises for Your Intuitive Heart*

"Pehrson and Mehrtens convert concepts that are usually reserved for cocktail party chatter or the therapist's couch into proactive tools that can assist business people to deal with the rapid changes we face today."—**John A. Thompson**, CEO, IMCOR, author, *The Portable Executive*

"In an increasingly complex society, we need tools to cope with the rapids of change. This book provides a deeply powerful tool for collaborative advantage in any organizational setting. *Intuitive Imagery* offers valuable insights into how to navigate corporations into the new millennium."—**Jacqueline Cambata**, CEO, Phoenix Chemical Limited

"This book is a powerful key for individuals who want to unlock their own treasure chest and bring forth their unique personal richness."—**John Hormann**, author and consciousness researcher

"I predict that techniques of intuitive imagery will form the basis for an entire new industry in the twenty-first century. Those who carefully study and apply the knowledge presented in this book will be well equipped for the challenges that lie ahead."—**Jeffrey Mishlove, Ph.D.**, president, Intuition Network, author, *The Roots of Consciousness*

INTUITIVE IMAGERY

INTUITIVE IMAGERY
A Resource at Work

JOHN B. PEHRSON
SUSAN E. MEHRTENS

Routledge
Taylor & Francis Group

LONDON AND NEW YORK

First published by Butterworth-Heinemann

This edition published 2011 by Routledge
2 Park Square, Milton Park, Abingdon, Oxon OX14 4RN
711 Third Avenue, New York, NY 10017, USA

Routledge is an imprint of the Taylor & Francis Group, an informa business

Library of Congress Cataloging-in-Publication Data

Pehrson, John B., 1950–
    Intuitive imagery : a resource at work / John B. Pehrson, Susan E. Mehrtens.
        p. cm.
    Includes bibliographical references and index.
    ISBN 0-7506-9805-5
    1. Management. 2. Intuition (Psychology) I. Mehrtens, Susan E., 1945– . II. Title
HD38.P394 1997
658—dc21   96-47499
                                                              CIP

British Library Cataloguing-in-Publication Data
A catalogue record for this book is available from the British Library.

To Jeanne Borei, my lovely wife and partner, who has been my inspiration, my strength, and a willing traveler in countless imaging sessions.

To our children, Ryan, Sean, Alan, John, and Jenny, who have believed in me when others did not and who are very talented intuitive imagers.

To Pauline Mehrtens and Hubert Avelange, for believing in the reality of the psyche and giving me the space to live by dreams and imagery.

To all those who use intuitive imagery to improve their lives.

Contents

Foreword

Most of us sense these days that some sort of cultural change is taking place. It involves coming to realize that the things of our lives are interconnected in subtle ways far beyond what we were taught in science class. It includes a shift in the way we perceive authority, away from the widely recognized experts and toward a kind of inner knowing that, again, is not explained by recognized scientific concepts. Twenty years ago the word *intuition* was not thought of as an ability of executives, and was almost never used for anyone else without being preceded by the adjective *feminine*.

One would not have expected to see this book by John Pehrson and Susan Mehrtens a couple decades ago. But present times are very different. It is widely recognized that we have these intuitive abilities, and books and seminars are easy to find that deal with "intuitive leadership," "intuition workbook," "awakening intuition," and so on. One welcome characteristic of the present book is that it doesn't put forth a recipe or a set of rules. It suggests a well-tested approach but invites you to trust that your own intuition can guide you to the best way for you. The book further hints that this matter of developing trust in your own intuition is perhaps one of the most important things to be learned in life.

There is one small point on which I would like to comment. In reading the book you may encounter and wonder about the authors' comments regarding "scientism." The more you learn about your own intuition, the more clear it will become that its characteristics are in no way "explained" by science. In fact they imply a picture of reality that does not fit with the scientific worldview at all. We all recognize that Western science is extremely effective at what it was developed for—that is, to explore aspects of reality that have to do with prediction, control, and the ability to devise manipulative technologies. However, there are other features of human experience—creativity, intuition, aesthetic sense, mind contribution to healing, spiritual sense—about which science can tell us little. That's not a criticism of scientists; it's merely a characteristic of science. Thus when the authors note that "scientism" is not a very good attitude with which to approach intuition, they don't mean anything negative about science or scientists; they simply mean to warn you not to limit your experience of reality by holding too tightly to the picture of reality contained within the present scientific worldview.

Scientists typically consider the appearance of consciousness and intuition to be epiphenomenal—to be explained away rather than being a causal factor. Because of the prestige of modern science, open-ended exploration of the potential scope and profundity of intuition becomes moderated by the desire to appear "scientific," and we are deprived of the freedom to appreciate the fullness of its mystery.

Anecdotal data show clearly that on occasion, the behind-the-scenes creative-intuitive mind dramatically exceeds the conscious analytical mind in brilliance. It has a feel for patterns that cannot be matched by the conscious mind. It may make use of information to which the individual could not have had access by ordinary means. Even such a simple intuitive task as calling up from memory a desired bit of information, given the vaguest of clues, is mystifying and defies a really satisfying scientific explanation. Ordinary, everyday intuition sometimes amazes us by what it comes up with.

A high respect for intuition has been spoken of in the past. Spiritual philosopher Jiddu Krishnamurti declared that: "Intelligence highly awakened is intuition, which is the only true guide in life." A far older source, Plotinus (in his letters to Flaccus) stated: "Knowledge has three degrees: opinion, science, illumination. The means or instrument of the first is sense; of the second, dialectic; of the third, intuition. To the last I subordinate reason. It is absolute knowledge founded on the identity of the mind knowing with the object known." Some have claimed a link between intuition and mysticism—the claimed mystical union or direct communion with ultimate reality. The boundary between intuitive and mystical knowing is sufficiently indistinct that it is probably more fruitful to consider them together than as separate faculties.

In the early stages of coming to trust your own intuition (which trust may have been eroded by your experiences in educational institutions) there may be confusion with regard to which voice you are hearing—the deep intuition or some aspect of the ego-mind, or perhaps some faint trace of early childhood training. As intuition is trusted enough to act upon, with following experience considered feedback, the ability will be developed to differentiate, in very subtle ways, the deep intuition. Pehrson and Mehrtens, in very discreet ways so they are not pushing you inappropriately, invite you to discover that such deep trust becomes an important aspect of mature living.

There is no doubt that intuitive leadership is a concept in which we are learning to put more and more faith. Using intuition in decision making can, no doubt, ultimately improve performance toward the "bottom line." But real leadership aims at more profound goals. Through intuitive connections we may find both deeper communion with others and deeper understanding of whatever situation in which we find ourselves.

There is another aspect of leadership that is too often neglected. In sharing responsibility for an organization you are investing your own life. Every human being harbors within the self a deep intuitive sense of purpose, of which he or she may be quite unaware. Far more important than reaching any external goal, such as material success and praise for superior management, is willing and acting in alignment with that inner sense. If one feels unsure that alignment is yet discovered, the best procedure is to will in accordance with one's inner sense anyway, and watch for the feedback that will reveal whether alignment is present or not. Leaders who do this find that more and more of their time and attention are placed on matters such as maintaining inner peace; focusing on quality of relationships; assisting others to develop and act appropriately; selecting appropriate goals for the organization; and playing the role of global statesperson—and further find that the necessary tasks of effective management end up somehow being accomplished, with ease and grace.

The adventure to which you are invited is one that in the end leads to great reward. And so it is time for us to end the Foreword and get on with the main task. Great journey!

Willis W. Harman
Institute of Noetic Sciences
Sausalito, California
July, 1996

[We were particularly pleased that Willis wrote the above foreword because he was, for both of us, a very special friend and inspiring guide to things intuitive and spiritual. A tireless teacher, mentor, scholar, and scientist, Willis devoted his life to revisioning science, expanding human potential, and helping people recognize their intuitive gifts. We are deeply in his debt and are just two among thousands of people around the world who mourned his death in January 1997. Knowing Willis as we did, we know there could be no better monument to his life than to have many more people discover and use the power of their intuition—*J.B.P.* and *S.E.M.*]

Acknowledgments

Over the many years we have been using, refining, teaching, and getting feedback on imagery, we have become indebted to many people. Foremost among our teachers is Magaly Rodriguez, who first introduced us to the power and potential of imagery while I (John) was still with Dupont. She remains an inspiration to us, and our treatment of intuitive imagery is a further development and elaboration of her concept of creative imagery.

I am also equally indebted to Carol Ann Liaros for her time and effort in training the early members of the SWAT team to awaken to our intuitive skills. Carol Ann gave us the confidence to go forward with what was a radical process, at the time, inside a conservative company. She was the first support for this book in telling me that I would one day become an important spokesman for the process.

I am deeply grateful to the members of the SWAT team for their enthusiasm, commitment, and courage to explore new frontiers in improving our businesses, even when there were those around who would have tarred and feathered us. To Bill Kopish, Janis Webb, Bill Ervin, and Jerry McKay, I want you to know you will always have a special place in my heart.

I am thankful to Herman Maynard who, for a brief time inside DuPont, helped to create an environment of tremendous hope, possibility, and potential. It was through his efforts that I first met Magaly Rodriguez and Carol Ann Liaros. And he has continued to be a source of inspiration.

My heartfelt thanks go out to Jacqui Cambata for her early support, excitement, and belief in the imaging process. Thanks also to the core team members of the Washington Chapter of the World Business Academy (WBA) Linda Morris, Peggy Stephens, and Mark Ciavardoni. Their support helped me take imaging beyond the boundaries of DuPont.

Other early supporters include John Thompson, Jim Schwarz, Anne Rarich, Jan Nickerson, Carol Frenier, and Ann Hyde, all of whom helped me have the confidence to move forward. A special thanks to both Jan and Carol for their efforts to review the earliest manuscript. Their comments and recommendations have been incorporated into the book.

My deepest thanks to Greta Hauck, Preston Jones, Cheryl Laurendeau, John and Lynda Ryan, John and Olga Franklin, Jim Foreman, Nancy McMorrow, and Louise Hauck for your support of the process, and for the stories and testimonials you sent.

I am indebted to Marilyn Saunders, who, through her own work in imaging, has expanded my understanding of the process.

Sue and I extend our deepest thanks and gratitude to our assistant editor, Stephanie Aronson, our production editor, Hilary Selby Polk, and our publisher, Karen Speerstra, for their interest and belief in the subject, and for seeing the "diamond in the rough" that was the original workbook on which this book is based.

Another thanks must go to the hundreds of people who have taken workshops with us, whose questions and problems with the process helped us refine our techniques and explanations. So many of you have been an inspiration to us that it is impossible to name all of you in this limited space.

A final thanks must go to our families, for their steadfast support, interest, tolerance, and forbearance through the long days and nights when writing this book absorbed our time: Jeanne, Ryan, Sean, Alan, Jenny, John, Pauline, Ruth, and Hubert.

Background

I

Introduction

1

Sit down before fact like a little child, and be prepared to give up every preconceived notion, follow humbly and to whatever abyss Nature leads, or you shall learn nothing.

T.H. Huxley

Imagine if you were able to

- Predict the performance of the market up to a year in advance
- Speed new product development by focusing human resources and money on only the winning candidates
- Identify unspoken customer needs
- Identify which of your competitors would soon leave the business
- Know the best time to approach your boss for a raise
- Tell in advance at which company to get a job, or when it is time to move on to greener pastures, and where to look for your new job
- Determine your unique mission in life

The truth is: You can!

You can do all this, and more, by using the simple, easy techniques of intuitive imagery.

Intuitive imagery is what this book is about. It is a whole-brain process that harnesses intuition in a reliable, disciplined way. In six succinct chapters (chapters 5–10), we give you all you need to know to be able to access the parts of your brain that know the future and can provide the guidance you need to live your life and run your business for maximum fun and profit.

Before we describe the intuitive imagery process and how to do it, we give you some of the cultural and scientific background (in chapters 2–4), so you can see how intuitive imagery is grounded in science and how this powerful technology makes possible whole-brain thinking and problem solving.

In the final chapters (11 and 12), we offer more than a dozen examples of how people from all walks of life have used intuitive imagery in practical ways, from solving health problems to identifying unspoken customer needs critical to strengthening the sales relationship.

Before getting into specifics, you might want a sample of what intuitive imagery looks like and how it works. So here's an example of how imagery was used in a high-volume *Fortune* 50 business to provide insights into competitors and their actions in the future. The following excerpt from an imaging research project shows the potential of intuitive imagery for assessing competitors' strengths and weaknesses.

Date: **June 21, 1989**

Intuitive Key: **The Fortune 50 Business for Whom the Imaging Is Being Done**

Guide: See a person and describe. Comment on his/her strengths and weaknesses. Imagine a brief, year-end 1989 headline.

Image: A tiger. Extremely powerful. It hunts when it feels the need to hunt and rests the remainder of the time. *Weaknesses:* The only life it has is hunting and resting. It uses a great deal of energy stalking its prey, then it has to rest again. So the tiger leads a very "basic" life. *Headline:* "Siberian tigers coming closer to extinction: Fewer than five are found in the wild"

Interpretation: This business is seen as the most powerful in the market (true). But a lot of energy is being expended in competitive battles (stalking its prey) to get new business. There are five major competitors, which is picked up by the imaging.

Intuitive Key 1: Competitor 1

Guide 1: See a person. Comment on his/her strengths and weaknesses. Imagine a year-end 1989 headline.

Image: A thin woman with red hair. Although she has the ability to overcome most difficulties, her weakness is that she is too sensitive. She is easily hurt and vulnerable. *Headline:* "Woman dies of heart attack"

Interpretation: The weakest of the competitors. There is a potential that they will exit the market by year-end 1989.

Result: This competitor did exit the market by the end of 1989, selling its converter-based business to the business for whom the imaging was done.

Intuitive Key 2: Japanese Competitors

Guide 2: See a person. Comment on his/her strengths and weaknesses. Imagine a year-end 1989 headline.

Image: A twenty-fourth century pilot. In the twenty-fourth century, humankind has moved into the solar system and lives on other planets. This pilot travels between them. He is helmeted but has very "intense eyes." *Strength:* His strength has something to do with the ability to pilot a huge spacecraft but is unclear. *Weakness:* He spends a lot of time traveling between planets, so he doesn't get to experience any of them very much. *Headline:* "Space pilot tests first hypercruiser: Flight ends in success/Cruiser to be certified within next three years"

Interpretation: The Japanese have new technology that may be a threat. The huge spacecraft may be the Japanese system of interrelated banks and businesses. Their weakness is long distribution lines. But they will act to shorten these distribution lines within the next three years (certification of the hypercruiser) through a joint venture or by building a manufacturing plant in the United States.

Results: On July 5, 1991, two years after the imaging was done, the *Journal of Commerce* announced a joint venture between Hoechst-Celanese (U.S.), Hoechst AG, their German parent company, and Mitsubishi Kasei Corporation, Mitsubishi Plastics Industries, and their Diafoil Company unit. A key part of the joint venture was establishing a U.S. company, Hoechst Diafoil Co., by January 1, 1992, to compete more effectively in the polyester film market. In addition, the Japanese company, Toyobo, is now [1995] building a polyester film plant in Rhode Island.

This example of intuitive imagery shows all the components, how the imagery is recorded, and the sorts of results imagery can provide.

We have taught intuitive imagery to thousands of people in the last seven years and have never found anyone unable to learn to do it, but some people are more familiar and comfortable than others with the components of intuitive imagery. If you want to assess your own comfort level with the process, we have provided a questionnaire for this purpose in Appendix 1.

More and more people every year are turning to intuitive imagery to deal with the challenges of modern life. This is understandable when you consider what is going on in the world. The social, economic, and cultural drivers behind the growing use of intuition are discussed in chapter 2.

The Emerging World

2

> ... the whole structure of our society does not correspond with the
> worldview of emerging thought.
>
> *Frijof Capra*

HMOs, NIEs, LBOs, MTV. Hoffices, the triple-squeeze, LANs and CAD, cyberspace, and the digerati. PNI and biopolitics,[1] flex-firms, designer currencies, advertorials, blended families. Downsizing, rightsizing, dumbsizing, and reengineering.

Welcome to the new borderless world of business, where billion-dollar deals are done in the space of nanoseconds, and computer databases give us daily doses of infoglut. Too many facts. Too little time. How is a business person to cope?

As we approach the new millennium, life is characterized by accelerating rates of social, political, and business change. We live with rapidly increasing complexity, uncertainty, environmental stress, and global conflict. Most of our ecosystems are in decline. Our cherished institutions are under attack. These are signs of the times. Anyone who has reflected for more than a moment on the state of the planet knows we have some tough problems to solve if we are to create a sustainable future, and it falls to business, as the world's most powerful and adaptable institution, to come up with many of the solutions.

Yet business itself is not immune to the larger forces at work in the world. If it is to be our hope for the future, business must successfully deal with its own sustainability issues. Many companies are emerging from the turmoil of rightsizing, restructuring, and reengineering to find temporarily improved profitability. But now, with a smaller and often less experienced workforce, companies must continue to reinvent themselves while grappling with the ongoing issues of employee commitment and productivity, lagging creativity, workforce diversity, tightening quality standards, environmental stewardship, global competition, and a host of other challenges. It is a time when the need for flexibility and rapid response have pushed our forecasting, planning, development, and decision-making systems to their absolute limits.

To paraphrase Einstein, neither the problems of the world nor the issues facing businesses today will be solved at the same level of thought at which they were created. Responding to today's challenges requires a willingness to be open to new, creative ways of thinking. Indeed, *we must begin to shift our beliefs about how we know what we know.* For this will also restructure how we do what we do.

There *is* hope on the horizon. Indeed, an overview of the emerging trends shows that new patterns of thinking are beginning to replace old mindsets. It is important to be aware of these trends as supports for a new way of being—both in business and in our personal lives. For example:

- More workers are taking back responsibility for their lives, careers, and retirement planning as the old paternalistic social contract unravels.[2]
- More people are reclaiming and internalizing authority— "authorizing their own lives"[3]—as respect for external authority figures and old-style bosses lessens.[4]
- More men and women are choosing to manifest their personal power by empowering others, as the old concept of power *over* others (power-as-domination) gives way to

power *with* others (power-as-dominion),[5] and competitive advantage slowly gives way to *collaborative* advantage.

- More businesses, governments and individuals are recognizing the ecologic reality of interconnectedness and interdependence—that everything really *is* connected to everything else.[6]
- Corporate culture is being transformed as the workplace is being "feminized" and feminine values, like egalitarianism, empathy, intuition, and feeling-based management styles, become more common.[7] Such trends are turning some corporations into "flex-firms,"[8] which are more hospitable places for people to work in.
- The scope of business is broadening, as new areas of focus compete with the bottom line for executive attention. In these days of strategic alliances, joint ventures, relationship selling, multiculturalism, concern for ethics and the "corporate soul," a single-minded focus on profits is not enough.[9]
- Technology is transforming the world of finance, as distinctions blur between banks and other financial services institutions,[10] new financial instruments (e.g., derivatives) arise,[11] and cold, hard cash becomes commoditized (in international financial arbitrage), informationalized (as intellectual currency), and personalized (in the form of "designer currencies").[12]
- More and more people are changing their attitudes about banking, regarding it more in terms of a relationship, rather than a process of exchange.[13]
- Nonfinancial navigational systems are becoming more and more important to business. New evaluative instruments like intellectual capital, social and resource accounting, and risk-management procedures are appearing to help business people cope with the new concerns and directions our society is taking.[14]
- There are growing calls for a "Third Way" economic system—something that is neither communism nor capitalism but is more suited to the twenty-first century world of rapid

change, sustainability, corporate accountability, and human-scale systems.[15]

- The sovereignty of nation states is being questioned and challenged on multiple fronts, from communication technologies like facsimile machines, the Internet, cell phones, and satellite television, to global currency arbitrageurs, who show no hesitation in humiliating governments (e.g., France's fate in August, 1993).[16]

- Science is shifting away from "scientism," a degenerate, rigid form of science marked by an almost exclusive reliance on rational, left-brain logic. Its building blocks of positivism, mechanism, reductionism, and materialism form the foundation for the worldview that has been in place since the Copernican revolution in the sixteenth century. Yet scientism is now giving way to a more open, "extended science" that is inclusive of the full range of human experience.[17] Because much of intuitive imaging draws on discoveries of new science, we shall examine this trend in detail in the following chapter.

- There is growing talk of a "metanoia," a basic change of consciousness, that is one aspect of a wider paradigm shift under way in global culture.[18] As Marilyn Ferguson stated in *The Aquarian Conspiracy*, "a new world is a new mind."[19] As we shift our awareness, the entire world changes.

The foundation of the worldview that has been in place for more than three hundred years is shifting. And it is not comfortable. Many of us may feel as though we are somehow out of balance, as if we were dancing on a slippery floor. Our tendency is to steady ourselves by holding on to what is safe and familiar. We wall ourselves off and try to close out the world. It is difficult to let go and keep a flexible stance. Yet our best chance of keeping our balance in a changing world is not to isolate ourselves from the changes happening around us. Rather it is to be aware of the fundamental rethinking of the major assumptions upon which our society rests. It is important, as the poet says, that "awake people be awake,"[20] or the emerging patterns may overwhelm us. It is in this context that intuitive imaging becomes an important tool.

Consciousness is changing, paradigms are shifting, time is accelerating, problems are becoming more and more complex, global competition is intensifying, and the very fundamentals of business are in flux. Our forecasting and planning systems seem to work less and less well. In negotiating these rapids of change in the 1990s, how indeed is a business person to cope?

Clearly not by using more of the same old left-brain, linear methods on which we have relied in the past. For 350 years we have exalted our "outer knowing" through objective reason. In the face of mounting global problems, we are like the proverbial crazy man who keeps on doing what he's always done, expecting each time to get different results. The new twist in the modern age is that we think we can escape the insanity if only we can do *more* of the same thing *faster* and with computers. Yet staying in our comfort zones will only produce the same old results. It is obvious that we are at a point where something must change.

The challenges of our emerging world cry out for new ways of thinking. We need nonlinear approaches that allow us to make better decisions faster. We need holistic techniques that integrate both reason and intuition to handle complex problems more effectively. We need powerful technologies that can give us an accurate bead on the future for reliable long-range planning. In short, we need to use more of our brain, in new ways, than we ever have before. Fortunately, at this juncture, science is turning up discoveries that make it possible for us to exploit a wider range of our abilities as human beings. We consider some of these discoveries in chapter 3.

NOTES

1. The abbreviations stand for, in order: health maintenance organization; newly industrializing economies (Hong Kong, Taiwan, Singapore, South Korea, Malaysia, Thailand, Indonesia, the Philippines); leveraged buy-outs; music television; home offices; local area networks; computer-assisted design; the digit literate, able to work with computers; psychoneuro-immunology.
2. Cf. Sontag 1992; Siegel 1986, 105–6; and Rowland 1992.
3. Keen 1992, 27.
4. Krieger 1973, 141–62.
5. Cf. Autry 1991, 14, 150; Sky 1993; Eisler 1987.
6. Cf. Commoner 1971, 33–46; Leary 1993; Stevens 1992; Storer 1956; Storer 1968; and Norton 1991.
7. Cf. Mandel 1993, 168; Naisbitt and Aburdene 1990, 229; Smith 1992, 123; Hilts 1993.
8. Toffler 1990.
9. Popcorn 1991, 159.
10. Hansell 1993; White 1992.
11. Greenspan 1992; Norris 1992; Saul 1992.
12. Stevenson 1992; Passell 1992; Gage 1993; Toffler 1990.
13. Jacobs 1991.
14. Cf. Chemical Bank 1992; Ekins 1986, 129–30.
15. Mollner 1988.
16. Wriston 1992a; Wriston 1992b; Hochschild 1993.
17. Steinfels 1993; Appleyard 1992, 2.
18. Cf. Naisbitt and Aburdene 1985; Naisbitt and Aburdene 1990; Ray and Rinzler 1993.
19. Ferguson (1980), 406.
20. Bly, Hillman, and Meade 1992, 233.

3

The Science Behind Intuitive Imagery

It takes at least fifty years before a major scientific discovery penetrates the public consciousness.

physicist Erwin Schrodinger

The popular understanding of how the world works has lagged behind the scientific discoveries that have fueled the technological revolution of the last fifty years. But more and more people are beginning to wake up to the misalignment between the structure of our society and the emerging worldview.[1] Collectively, we are becoming aware that a "new science" has been emerging in the twentieth century that has overturned most of the foundations of the old Newtonian model of reality that we were taught in high school. The bad news is that many of our old beliefs about what is "real" no longer fit what our leading scientists now know to be true. The good news is that "new science" has the potential to free us to use much more of our innate human capabilities. This is heady stuff with the potential to change the way we see the world around us and, as a result, choose to operate in it.

Intuitive imaging is a tool forged from the furnace of the new science and built upon the foundation of its discoveries. It is

13

a tool that once learned, can provide access to accelerated whole-brain learning, increased creativity, and deep insight. Before considering the scientific underpinnings of intuitive imaging, we need to first clarify what we mean by "old" science and "new" science. We will do this by explaining the governing principles of old science. This is important because these principles still form the basis for the dominant worldview that defines today's business environment. We have inherited its blindspots and limitations. To help break free of these mind funnels that constrict our thinking, we will first recap the discoveries that have led to a new scientific worldview and then draw their relevance to business and the use of expanded human capabilities like intuitive imaging.

THE PARADIGM OF CONVENTIONAL ("OLD") SCIENCE

With *old science*, or *scientism*, we refer to the degenerate form of current science,[2] degenerate because in its dogmatism it has ceased to be an open-minded search for truth. The cardinal rule of science is open-minded acceptance of *all* of reality, "even that which it cannot understand, explain, that for which no theory exists, or which cannot be measured, predicted, controlled or ordered."[3] Over time, scientism has turned its back on the hunger for a direct experience of reality that the early men of science demonstrated. As a result, it has created blindspots for itself as it has hidden behind a rigid mask of objectivity and analysis to screen out and reject experimental evidence contrary to its own beliefs.

Scientism is committed to a Newtonian model of reality. That is, it is mechanistic, built around the model of the world as a machine,[4] with rigid laws of cause and effect. The Newtonian world is the deterministic world of the "clockwork Universe," a linear world in which time, space, and distance are discrete dimensions.[5] We are, according to this view, like individual billiard balls, separate from one another, rolling through life reacting to the people and events that strike us. This is not to say that there is anything wrong with Newtonian science—as far as it goes. It is very effective for dealing with the macroscopic, tangible reality of the physical plane. Indeed, Newtonian science proved adequate for many decades, particularly in dealing with the inanimate world.[6] But clearly, the world is not a machine. And we are not billiard balls.

Newtonian science not only is mechanistic; it also is positivistic—rooted in mathematics and enamored of numbers.[7] Any business person familiar with "analysis paralysis" inside a large corporation can relate to the "let's-run-the-numbers-one-more-time" syndrome, and the "bottom line" mentality. Quantification is a key process in scientism, partly because it allows "objective inquiry."[8] Many positive results flow from quantification, to be sure. Appropriate metrics are critical to improving product quality or in the financial management of a business. The unfortunate result of this positivistic bent, however, is that scientism became deeply biased against any phenomena *not* amenable to measurement and mathematical treatment, for example, "soft" subjects like philosophy, literature, or issues of values. In other words, if you can't measure it, it's not "real." But how do you measure the width of an idea, or the volume of the imagination? How do you calculate the cosine of the soul, or weigh the beauty of a sunset? In its objectivity, conventional science purports to be value-free,[9] yet tends to disparage those areas of life (like the value of a river ecosystem, the worth of a human life, or the power of love) that cannot be calculated in numbers, dollars, or cents. This bias against the intangible values of life has carried over into our businesses as well.

Another feature of old science is its reliance on reductionism,[10] which uses left-brain analytical techniques to solve problems by reducing them to their constituent parts. The undergirding belief of the reductionist approach is that once you understand the component parts, you have mastered the whole. This might be true with chicken nuggets at the local fast food place, where "parts is parts." It may also be true in some of the physical sciences, like chemistry. But it is most definitely not true in higher-order sciences like ecology or medicine. Reductionism ignores the principle of holism—that complex living systems (like human bodies, ecosystems, weather patterns, or organizations) are more than the mere sum of their parts. Such systems have "emergent properties"[11] (like coherence, interdependence, mind, or morphogenesis) that reductionism fails to consider.

Of all its founding tenets, perhaps the most severe bias in scientism is its materialism, the exclusive focus on the physical. In this view, only the tangible, material universe is real, "a universe controlled by fixed physical laws and blind chance. . . . Life and consciousness are totally identical to physical processes, and arise from chance interactions of blind, physical forces."[12] In other words, if you can't see it, hear it, taste it, touch it, or smell it, then it's not real. Taken to its extremes in scientism, this also means that life and consciousness have no objective purpose, meaning or destiny.[13] Intangible realities, like creativity, imagination, intuition, and even consciousness are ignored, or dismissed.[14] Just how much our culture has absorbed this bias is obvious from the frequency with which we hear the stock dismissive phrase, "Oh, it's only your imagination." The clear implication is that "it" (whatever "it" might be) is not real, not worthy of attention or credence. Hence we grow up in a culture that disparages any higher meaning or purpose in the world, and would sacrifice our creative and imaginative powers to the god of objectivity and rationalism.

Criticism of "old science" and recognition of its limitations arose, ironically, from within science itself, particularly in the ranks of the premier science, physics.[15] In the history of science, physics has always been the leader, and it began an assault on old science in the mid-nineteenth century, with the work of Michael Faraday in magnetism.[16]

KEY DISCOVERIES IN NEW SCIENCE

Faraday's studies of magnets and the behavior of iron filings in their presence led him to develop the concept of invisible lines of magnetic force. Two decades later James Clerk Maxwell took Faraday's work further, to show how electricity and magnetism are bound together, so that a magnetic field is really an electromagnetic field.[17] Maxwell discovered that electromagnetic fields result from the charged nature of particles. These invisible charges emit disturbances in space that act on other particles at a distance through invisible, nonmaterial fields. Because the universe is everywhere made up of such charged atomic particles, it follows that the entire universe is filled with invisible force fields that interpenetrate and interact. If this were not so, we could not have developed television, cell phones, or satellite communications. This electromagnetic field theory was the first chink in the materialist armor of conventional science, for it demonstrated that reality is not only material—electromagnetic fields are real but intangible.

The second assault came from Einstein's special theory of relativity. Among his many achievements in physics, Einstein refined Maxwell's equations dealing with the effects of electromagnetism[18] in his theory that all motion in the universe is not absolute but relative to some chosen frame of reference. The discovery of relativity revealed that many "common sense" Newtonian concepts were erroneous; for example, space and time are not separate, discrete entities, but are smoothly linked and part of a larger whole that Einstein called "space-time," a four-dimensional continuum.[19] Mass and energy also are not discrete but share a relationship (energy being the product of mass times the speed of light squared, the famous equation $E = mc^2$). Mass—a human body, for example—is energy.[20] We are fundamentally energy systems, living in a universe in which time is relative. Two observers will order events differently in time if they move with different velocities relative to observed events. This Einsteinian discovery posed a difficult challenge to determinism (effect follows cause) and to claims about the objectivity of positivism.

Positivism was similarly challenged by Heisenberg's deduction of the uncertainty principle. In 1927 Werner Heisenberg drew from nuclear theory the principle that it is impossible to determine simultaneously both the exact position and speed of any particle. An observer could *choose* to observe one or the other, position or speed, but not both. This principle (which initially appalled Einstein) led to the weakening of the Newtonian concept of cause and effect and destroyed the deterministic principle of scientism.[21] It also revealed the key role played by the scientist as observer: We choose what we observe. As one physicist recently noted,

> . . . it is precisely how we observe that creates the reality we perceive. Change the 'how' of it and you change the 'what' of it. In other words, change how you see and think about yourself, and you change what is actually present in the world.[22]

Under the impact of the uncertainty principle, the claim of scientism that it is objective and value-free crumbles. This is because the mind influences events through a "causal influence on the probability of their occurring."[23] In other words, there is no such thing as a truly objective observer. What we experience, whether it is in a scientific experiment or in life, has a great deal to do with what we expect.

Another discovery in physics that challenged the old scientific paradigm is holography. Dennis Gabor won the Nobel Prize in physics in 1971 for developing the theory of holography. In a series of experiments in 1947, he demonstrated the possibility of using a coherent beam of light to regenerate the original wave pattern of an object, producing an information-rich three-dimensional image.[24] After laser beams were invented in the 1960s, Emmet Leith and Juris Upatnicks applied Gabor's theories to the construction of holograms. Soon other scientists were applying the concept beyond photography. Karl Pribram, for example, took over the hologram as a model of how the brain processes information,[25] and David Bohm developed a theory of the holographic universe.[26] These models drew upon the unique property of holograms: any piece of a hologram will reconstruct the entire image. In other words, every part contains and has access to the whole in a condensed form. There is no space-time dimension in holographic reality.

The discovery of holograms offers several challenges to old science. First, it indicates that primary reality exists in a domain beyond time and space that is everywhere interconnected. Second, it posits the brain as an organ interpreting a holographic universe. Third, it tells us that with our eyes we see not objective reality but a mathematical construct made by our brain as it interprets frequencies from a more fundamental dimension that transcends space and time. This is a striking concept that has the power to completely reorder how we view the world.

We might be tempted to stop with the sweeping implications of holography, yet there is more, equally compelling evidence that the world is not as we have been taught to perceive it. Bell's theorem provided another subversion of old science. This discovery derived from a 1935 experiment by Albert Einstein, Boris Podolsky, and Nathan Rosen (called EPR, for their three names) that seemed to contradict physical law. It indicated that observation of the location of one particle instantaneously provided information about the location of another. The puzzle here was with "instantaneously": How could two particles be related so closely that information could travel between them faster than the speed of light? In 1964, John Bell took up this puzzle, proving that subatomic particles are connected everywhere, even at a distance, instantaneously, and at all times. Bell's theorem states that information can indeed travel faster than light.[27] Because everything material, including each of us, is made up of these subatomic particles, this discovery undercuts reductionism. We are not discrete units but are all connected, affecting each other, even over large distances—even if we can't explain how. This influence we have on other entities is profound, extending over generations, as we shall see when we turn to discoveries in the biological sciences.

Physics has not been the only scientific discipline to challenge the assumptions of scientism. Particularly in recent decades it has been joined by the biological and neurological sciences and by the human sciences. There have been many discoveries. We can consider only a representative sampling from these fields.

We will take the biological sciences first. Bell's theorem revealed how subatomic particles—and by extension, everything made of these particles—are connected in ways that transcend space and time. In morphogenetic field theory, this mutual influence is seen as even more profound than Bell thought, being not merely instantaneous but extending over generations. We noted earlier how electromagnetic fields affect us. But they are not the only such fields. In the 1970s, drawing on ancient concepts and modern science, Rupert Sheldrake proposed the theory of *morphogenetic* fields, invisible, organized, *causative* fields that act as blueprints for the forms (Greek *morphos*) and behaviors of biological species (including humans).[28] Like electromagnetic fields and the intraparticle information dealt with in Bell's theorem, morphogenetic fields function independently of space and time. Sheldrake hypothesized that the morphogenetic process is accretive: it builds by the accumulated actions of members of a species. When one member learns a new behavior, the causative field shifts slightly. If the new learned behavior is repeated long enough, by more members of the species, a "morphic resonance" is created that affects the entire species, leading to a change in the behavior of all members. The entire species is then able to learn faster, because the new form resides in the morphogenetic field and patterns behavior.[29] Long-term studies of primate and rat populations have borne out Sheldrake's theory.[30] This theory has tremendous implications for business in creating "learning communities," and for shifting from *competitive* advantage to *collaborative* advantage.

In the neurosciences, discoveries of brain hemisphericity have shown the biases of scientism in stark relief. The split-brain research of Roger Sperry and his associates has explicated the different processing styles of our left and right brains. In a series of studies of brain-damaged people over nearly 30 years,[31] Sperry showed that the left brain is the domain of logic, verbal processing, mathematical reasoning, and intellectual and analytical functioning. It is verbal, sequential (linear), time-bound, and masculine-yang. It is the realm of "old science." Although we value and stress this side of our brain most in Western culture, it makes up a small amount of actual brain cells (roughly two billion). Fifty times as large is the right-brain–unconscious part of our brain. Sperry's studies showed that the right brain (long thought to be "stupid") is actually very active, handling such tasks as spatialization, pattern recognition, facial discrimination, nonverbal processing, and visual awareness. The right brain is intuitive, emotional, creative, musical, timeless, and feminine-yin. While the left brain analyzes, the right brain sees wholes and synthesizes. While the left seeks control, the right brain seeks relationship. Sperry showed that human consciousness is the sum of both brains. We have access to both sets of skills. Yet largely because of the bias of scientism toward linearity, logic, reason, and analysis, we have ignored and disparaged one-half of our human information-processing potential. If we are to meet the challenges of the twenty-first century, we must learn to become whole-brain thinkers.

Other challenges to scientism come from discoveries in newer sciences, such as psychoneuroimmunology (PNI). Beginning in the 1970s, neuroscientists, biologists, and medical clinicians began to cross disciplinary lines, to create this new subspecialty that deals with the integrated, holistic functioning of the mind (psycho-), nervous system (neuro-), and immune system (immunology). Practitioners of this new discipline speak of studying the "bodymind,"[32] in recognition of the intimate, irreducible connections between mental activities and physical function. In this new way of thinking, "mind" is an "emergent property"[33] not of the brain only (as materialist scientism would have it) but of the entire being. PNI research shows how the mind (which in the larger sense includes emotions, fears, etc.) affects the body, and how neuropeptides (chemical secretions from glands throughout the body that act as messengers) affect thinking and the functioning of the body. From sophisticated experiments PNI researchers have shown the reality of "gut feelings." Digestive peptides are active agents in our mental processing. In fact, from PNI discoveries, it seems that we "think" as much with our stomachs and intestines as with our brains.[34] PNI has produced many novel discoveries that challenge old ways of thinking. For example, the brain is a gland[35]; hormones are the stuff of thought; the mind is not localized in the brain, but exists throughout the body[36]; and what we think about can influence our entire physical system.

This is the basis of adjunctive healing therapies, in use for more than twenty years by a wide range of medical practitioners and clinicians, including Carl and Stephanie Simonton,[37] Yale surgeon Bernard Siegel,[38] and psychiatrist Gerald Epstein.[39] These practitioners have discovered that specific mental imagery, practiced repeatedly in a supportive atmosphere and under the guidance of medical professionals, has considerable healing impact, even in serious cases of cancer, heart disease, tuberculosis, autoimmune diseases, and other forms of illness.

Other discoveries, in disciplines beyond PNI and medicine, have taken this even further: Your mind has the power to influence not only your own body but also others' bodies. It can change not only the future but also the past. Carefully designed parapsychological research conducted over 30 years at several U.S. universities have revealed the extraordinary power of the mind. Some of the most noteworthy of these studies have been conducted by physicist Robert Jahn at the Princeton Engineering Anomalies Research laboratory.[40] Jahn and his team spent years recording the experiences of research subjects told to use their minds to skew the results of random event generating machines. Subjects were asked to get one result or another, not only for runs in the future but also for runs in the past.[41] Jahn discovered that as long as the results were not observed after being run by the machine, his subjects could change the results days later. He concluded that

> under certain circumstances human consciousness can interact with physical systems to broaden their observable behavior beyond chance expectation.[42]

This interaction is independent of time.

Modern discoveries have challenged scientism and created a new opportunity for ancient wisdom to resurface as credible.

From one of the oldest areas of research come more such discoveries. The nature and functions of the human energy system have been studied by the Chinese for thousands of years, providing the basis for acupuncture and acupressure as well as the philosophical underpinnings of the Chinese theory of yin and yang. Western sources from the ancient Greek Pythagoras[43] to the eighteenth century Frenchman Antoine Mesmer[44] have also observed and used human energy fields for healing purposes. In our own century, the English physician Walter Kilner[45] and the U.S. physician G. W. Crile[46] treated people with disease by means of manipulation of the aura. The Russian team of Semyon and Valentina Kirlian created a photographic process that captures the bioenergy field or "aura" of living objects on film.[47] It has been only in the last 20 years that healing by means of auric manipulation has become more mainstream. For example, Dr. Mehmet Oz, a cardiac surgeon at Columbia Presbyterian Hospital in New York, incorporates the "medicinal power of chi"[48] into his treatment of patients with heart disease. Because of the labors of teacher-practitioners like Dr. John Pierrakos,[49] Barbara Brennan,[50] Dr. Robert Jaffe, Rosalyn Bruyere, Michael Mamas, Dolores Krieger,[51] and Jason Shulman, hundreds of people have been trained in techniques that use human energy fields to access universal mind to foster healing on both physical and spiritual levels.[52]

Research on creativity and intuition provides more examples of discoveries that illustrate the limitations of scientism. In investigating this subject—which old, positivistic science disparages—we face the irony that one of the richest sources of examples of the operation of intuition is the history of science itself. From Poincaré's mathematical insights on the omnibus,[53] to Kekulé's discovery of the benzene ring in a dream,[54] and Otto Loewe's dream solutions two nights in a row for the action of the nerve fiber,[55] science is replete with examples of intuition— flashes of insight, momentary visions of solutions—turning up the right answer. We examine intuition in depth in chapter 4. For our purposes here, we need only note that the fostering and evaluation of intuition and creativity have been studied at length by a wide array of researchers.[56] The four-step process they have identified—preparation, incubation, illumination, and verification[57]—has analogues in the intuitive imaging process, as we explain in chapter 6.

When presented with discoveries like these, from the physical, biological, human, and neurological sciences, scientism has reacted with its typical close-minded prejudice,[58] dismissing the investigators (many of whom are Nobel laureates) as crackpots or "mystics." But it is scientism, not these thousands of researchers, that is wrong. As this is becoming obvious to more and more people, we are witnessing the rise of a new type of science, an "extended"[59] or "post-modern" science,[60] a method of inquiry, discovery and shared interpretation that goes beyond the determinism, materialism, positivism, and reductionism of the old, petrified scientism to accommodate the myriad new discoveries described earlier. New science admits a wider spectrum of reality than quantifiable facts. It includes insights and nonlinear, right-brain ways of knowing and melds logic and intuition. It recognizes that objectivity is a myth,[61] because (as the "observer effect" in physics tells us) the observer influences what is seen. New science operates not under the machine model but under a holistic, organismic model that views the whole as more than the sum of the parts.[62] It emphasizes synthesis as much as analysis and is value-laden, looking not merely for the facts but for the meaning behind them.

THE SCIENCE BEHIND INTUITIVE IMAGING

How do these sometimes startling discoveries of new science relate to intuitive imaging? Let's briefly tour these scientific achievements again, this time drawing their implications and relevance as the science behind intuitive imaging.

Electromagnetic Field Theory   Faraday and Maxwell demonstrated that nonmaterial electromagnetic fields are real. Every object made of atomic particles (everything, including each of us) creates an electromagnetic field. These fields can interact with and affect each other across both space and time. Therefore we affect each other in subtle ways through the interaction of our own fields. Anyone who has felt someone staring at him or her from across the room has experienced this effect. When we work with intuitive imaging, the fact that we can create accurate and useful images for someone else is due in part to the reality of electromagnetic fields.

The Theory of Relativity   Einstein showed that time is relative. Clock time is not the time of our experience. Three seconds spent holding a hot cinder feels a lot longer than three seconds spent licking an ice cream pop; thirty seconds in a car out of control can seem like a lifetime as your life flashes before your eyes. We function in part outside the Newtonian framework of time and space, particularly in the mental realm of images and beliefs. This is one explanation for how in intuitive imaging we can tap into the future.

Heisenberg's Uncertainty Principle   Heisenberg demonstrated that life involves choices, conscious or unconscious. His principle puts choice as a central issue in existence. The observer effect says we *choose* to see certain things and not others. We make these choices (if they are conscious) by the exercise of our free will and under the influence of our beliefs. In other words, *believing is seeing,* not the other way around. For example, if we believe in lack and limitation, we choose to see a glass half empty. But if we believe in supply and abundance, we see the same glass half full. In either case, we will act in a way that supports our belief. This discovery of new science reminds us that a key part of how we interpret the world lies in the choices we make. If you are anchored to a materialistic worldview, then you will have difficulty accepting the validity of an intuitive process. On the other hand, if you are open to the discoveries of new science, you will understand intuitive imaging as an example of our natural human abilities.

Bell's Theorem Everything is connected to everything else, instantaneously and at any distance. This includes us as human beings. We are not separate entities, so what happens to one of us affects all of us, and what happens in the world happens in our own lives as well. Because we are all connected, our thoughts and images at some level also are linked. By extension, our thoughts and images can travel instantaneously over distances and can be received by others.

Holography The quintessential aspect of a hologram is that each part, no matter how small, contains the entire hologram. Neurosurgeon Karl Pribram demonstrated that our brains store memories holographically. Physicist David Bohm extended the holographic principle to include the entire universe, meaning that every constituent part of the universe contains all of it in some condensed form. Each organism (e.g., you or I) represents the universe, and each of us has access to all the information in the whole, under certain conditions. In physical systems, this "condition" is the coherent light of the laser. In the mental realm, the analogue to laser light is the coherence created by intuitive imaging techniques (which we discuss in chapter 5). Holography also tells us that our inner images are as "real" as our outer reality. Moreover, the part of the universe we represent is a mirror of our inner images and beliefs. So by changing these images, we can produce change in the outer world, when we invest our images with sufficient desire and faith (i.e., energy). Mental images may be more fundamental than physical reality: what we imagine and visualize affects outer life events. Strongly held images can become real, especially if we hold them in a coherent (transcendental) state, and invest them with belief, desire, and faith. Holography draws on electromagnetic field theory in its recognition that every entity in the universe is primarily energy or vibration, human beings no less than atomic particles. When we use mental images, we can interact with this vibrational energy to produce real change in our lives. The most powerful images, universal symbols (what Jungian psychology calls "archetypes") are holographic in nature: They provide access to or an entry point into a whole spectrum of life, or into an era or a culture about which our rational minds may know nothing. Indeed, our deepest forms of knowing come not from the rational mind but from intuitions, dreams, reveries, and feelings.

Morphogenetic Field Theory   As human beings, we are influenced by the morphogenetic field of the species *homo sapiens.* As any one of us learns we all are positively affected. Beyond the individual, organizations also have morphogenetic fields that are created, sustained, and evolved by the actions of the members of the organization (e.g., a corporate culture). Human morphogenetic fields are created as much by mental images as by behaviors. When we tap into the morphogenetic field, we can access images that contain information beyond what we think we can know.

Split-brain Research   Because of the union of our left and right brains, we have a wide range of abilities, intuitive as well as rational, emotional as well as intellectual. With fifty times the amount of brain cells devoted to right-brain activities, we have much larger mental potentials if we use technologies that allow us to access this nonverbal half of our brains. Research has proved that whole-brain approaches to problem-solving are much more effective and powerful than use of only the left-brain rationality advocated by scientism. Intuitive imaging is a whole-brain approach that allows the right brain to be heard. In the intuitive imaging process the right brain is engaged first to produce images that get beneath the rational mind. Only then are the logic and analysis of the left brain brought in to provide interpretation and validation. In this way, the right brain is not shut out, as usually happens with traditional techniques of investigation. Rather it is a balanced approach that utilizes the strength of both hemispheres of the brain—intuition and reason.

Psychoneuroimmunology   The multidisciplinary science of PNI traces how feelings influence our bodily functions. Because our bodies are made of vibrating energies, our moods, images, and beliefs create changes in our energy field. Because the electromagnetic fields emanating from our bodies overlap and interpenetrate, our moods, images, and beliefs also affect others, without the use of words, and independent of the constraints of Newtonian time and space. Intuitive imaging makes explicit these effects we have on others.

Human thoughts and imagery have an effect not only on other people but also on the general environment and living things in it, like plants. In a seminal pioneering book,[63] Chris Bird and Peter Tompkins demonstrated that plants respond to specific human thoughts. This is true for both thoughts directed to the plants and nondirected thoughts. When tending plants, for example, the researchers who held thoughts of love or nurturance toward the plants saw those plants grow faster and be healthier. Negative thoughts resulted in stunted growth and shortened life spans. The nondirected response was just as powerful: Plants placed in a room where people were crying, grieving, or angry did not thrive or began to wilt, whereas plants in an atmosphere of love, joy, or happiness grew faster, were stronger, and produced more blooms.[64] The old English idiom "love blooms" apparently is not merely a metaphor. Love really does cause plants to bloom.

Parapsychological Research   "Mind over matter" is no trite phrase. Mental intention *can* skew the performance of machines to produce specific results. Parapsychological research has shown through definitive experimental results that we *do* communicate nonverbally and at a distance through our images and thought energy. Each of us is a sender and receiver. It appears to be a natural human ability.

Human Energy Field Research   Via the aura, human beings carry the vibrational effects of thoughts and images into physical reality to affect other people or the general environment. Through the human energy field we are all connected, both with other people and with levels above the physical plane.

Intuition and Creativity Research   Creativity is not a chance thing, nor is intuition an unusual gift reserved only for psychics and seers. We all have it, and it can be consciously nurtured, fostered, and cultivated. Research in these areas has shown that the more intuition is valued, used, tested, and trusted, the more prominent and reliable it becomes. As a vital part of the scientific process, intuition has been central to our evolution as a species. Intuitive imaging helps people trust in their intuition by giving clear and explicit examples of its accuracy and power.

Sports Performance Research   Much research has been done on the experiences of countless athletes and sports figures who have used imaging processes to optimize athletic performance. Optimal sports performance research has become a field in itself in the last two decades, amalgamating knowledge from psychology, physiology, and metaphysics to boost the performance of professional athletes and Olympic contenders. Jack Nicklaus, for example, always uses imagery to improve his game, even in practice sessions:

> I never hit a shot, not even in practice, without having a very sharp, in-focus picture of it in my head. It's like a color movie. First I "see" the ball where I want it to finish, nice and white and sitting up high on the bright green grass. Then the scene quickly changes and I "see" the ball going there: its path, trajectory, and shape, even its behavior on landing. Then there is a fadeout, and the next scene shows me making the kind of swing that will turn the previous images into reality.[65]

Similarly, Chris Evert uses visualization techniques to practice tennis matches. Arnold Schwarzenegger and Frank Zane held images of the body they desired while they trained for body-building championships.[66] These are but a few of the many sports figures who attribute their success, in part, to the use of imaging techniques. While these techniques may seem new, they are actually ancient. The knowledge that the inner images we hold affects our outer reality goes back thousands of years.[67]

Psychology Intuitive imagery also draws on the field of psychology, particularly analytical and transpersonal psychologies. Analytical psychology, also known as "archetypal" psychology,[68] was founded by Carl Jung, a Swiss psychiatrist whose empirical studies of mental patients led him to develop the concept of the "collective unconscious," that deeper layer of unconsciousness in every person that contains "archetypes" or "patterns of psychic perception"[69] common to every human being, regardless of sex, race, age, or culture. In Jung's theory, we all resonate with these archetypes (e.g., the Divine Child, the Great Mother, the Wise Old Man, the Trickster)[70] and share a basic psychological matrix out of which our personal consciousness grows. Much as Bell's theorem suggests, we are all connected, not only through particle energy fields but through the very constitution and content of our minds. We all are a part of a shared consciousness and hence can access it for information. The archetypes that exist in the collective unconscious are energy symbols that represent principal ideas. Focusing on them consciously can produce powerful resonance in both individuals and groups, which can be helpful in fostering insight, growth, and transformation. The intuitive imaging process draws on the wisdom in the collective unconscious and employs archetypal symbols, as we describe in detail in chapters 5 and 9.

CONCLUSION

Intuitive imaging is based on many recent discoveries in science, discoveries that are part of the new science that is challenging the current, degenerate form of science called *scientism*. If some of these discoveries seem bizarre, we need to remember that the Newtonian view has dominated science, and our culture, for more than two hundred years, whereas new science is but a few decades old. It will take a while for the new morphogenetic fields to be built up, when the new perspectives will seem less strange.

Meanwhile, we can tap into the potential of these discoveries and enjoy the benefits of the technologies it spawns, like intuitive imaging, *if we believe we can and choose to do so.* We use italics deliberately. The old saw "I'll believe it when I see it" is backward: You will see the merit in new science when you first are willing to believe it. We can believe in the new realities of our world more readily when we understand and experience how they work in practice. Just what intuitive imaging is and how it works is the subject of Part II.

NOTES

1. Ferguson 1980, 47.
2. Steinfels 1993; Appleyard 1992, 2.
3. Dossey 1993, 1694.
4. Metzner 1993, 9.
5. Appleyard 1992, 33.
6. Ibid., 43.
7. Ibid., 59.
8. Ibid., 176–7.
9. Ibid., 244; cf. Harman 1993, 15–6.
10. Davies 1993.
11. Feigl 1973, 548–9.
12. Breton and Largent 1991, 10–11.
13. Ibid.
14. Harman 1993, 16; cf. Augros and Stanciu 1984, xiv.
15. Augros and Stanciu 1984, xv.
16. Asimov 1982, 318.
17. Ibid., 455.
18. Ibid., 675.
19. Ibid.
20. Ibid.
21. Ibid., 784.
22. Wolf 1991, 194.
23. Sheldrake 1995, 47; Sheldrake 1995, 47.
24. Asimov 1982, 775.
25. Wolf 1984, 154–5.
26. Friedman 1994, 31–73.
27. Wolf 1984, 49–50.
28. Cf. Sheldrake 1981; Sheldrake 1988.
29. Sheldrake 1981, 183–98.
30. Sheldrake cites some of these studies in 1981, 103–7, 130–3, 185–91, 196–9.
31. Cf. Sperry 1964; Sperry 1968; Gazzaniga 1976; Gazzaniga and LeDoux 1978.

32. Pert 1987, 79.
33. Ibid., 87–8.
34. Snyder 1980, 979–81.
35. Bergland 1985, 92, 121.
36. Pert 1987, 88.
37. Simonton, Simonton, and Creighton 1978.
38. Siegel 1986.
39. Epstein 1989.
40. Jahn reports the findings of his team in Jahn and Dunne 1987.
41. Cited in Dossey 1993.
42. Jahn and Dunne 1987, 277.
43. Brennan 1987, 30.
44. Tompkins and Bird 1973, 19.
45. Kilner 1965, 3.
46. Tompkins and Bird 1973, 188.
47. Ostrander and Schroeder 1974, 59.
48. Oz was the subject of the American Agenda on the ABC Evening News January 11, 1996. This phrase was used by Peter Jennings as he introduced the segment; cf. Pollack 1995, D1.
49. Tompkins and Bird 1973, 210–1.
50. Cf. Brennan 1987; Brennan 1993.
51. Krieger is the founder of the practice of therapeutic touch, described in Krieger 1979.
52. As a cost-saving measure, more health maintenance organizations and insurance companies are beginning to cover alternative health care therapies; cf. Hilts 1995, 10; Egan 1996, 10.
53. Cited in Harman and Rheingold 1984, 28.
54. Cited in ibid., 41.
55. Asimov 1982, 645.
56. Cf. Koestler 1964; Harman and Rheingold 1984.
57. Harman and Rheingold 1984, 24–8.
58. Appleyard 1992, 214–5.
59. Harman 1993.
60. This is David Griffin's term for new science.
61. Ricci 1995, 10.
62. Blakeslee 1995, 10.
63. Tompkins and Bird 1973.
64. Ibid.
65. Quoted in Murphy 1992, 444.
66. Ibid., 444–5.
67. Talbot, 1991, 221–223.
68. Hopcke 1989, 13.
69. Ibid.
70. Ibid., 15.

II

What Is Intuitive Imagery?

Intuition and Imagery

4

> ... the rise of civilization in the last 2000 years reads like a history of the social suppression of visualization and therefore a denial of one of our most basic mental processes. For visualization *is* the way we think. Before words, images were.
>
> *Don Gerrard*

Intuitive imagery would never have been developed if the attitudes of our culture about scientism had not changed, making the components of intuitive imaging—intuition and imagery—"respectable" and widely studied. In this chapter, we define intuition and imagery and trace the evolving role they have been playing in our culture.

INTUITION

The word *intuition* refers to a form of spontaneous knowing without the conscious use of logic or analytical reasoning.[1] It is a way of knowing that transcends time and space.[2] Given the left-brain bias of Western culture, we usually think of "intuition" as something mental, a "brain skill"[3] that fosters faster decision making, but the history of the word in English reveals richer meanings, for example:

35

- Intuition as physical—the "gut reaction" or "knowing in the cells" that produces changes in physiologic processes, such as stomach or intestinal sensations, muscle twinges, changes in heartbeat or breathing.[4]
- Intuition as emotional—the instant "reading" of a person or situation with holistic awareness or sensitivity to the feeling context of the moment.[5]
- Intuition as a personality orientation. C. G. Jung, the Swiss psychiatrist, formulated a theory of personality "types" with four "functions": thinking, feeling, intuition, and sensation. Everyone manifests one of these as his or her "superior" function. The person who has intuition as the superior function tends to see things in wholes, to take in information all of a piece, to think in leaps. He or she gets flashes of insight or quick perception of patterns. The sensate person, by contrast, tends to take in information in linear steps, focusing on details and gathering them together to create, eventually, the big picture that the intuitive person sees all at once.[6] Sensation types comprise about 75% of the U.S. public, intuitives about 25%.[7]
- Intuition as an internal mode of daily existence. Floyd Bloom and his research group at the Scripps Institute have discovered that there is a regular alternation of the dominance of our two nostrils as we breathe throughout each day. When the left nostril predominates, the right side of the brain comes to prominence, and we can then be said to move into an "intuitive mode." This discovery reveals that we all have a natural intuitive way of being that alternates automatically with our rational, left-brain way of being.[8]
- Intuition as a mediator. Benjamin Libet and his colleagues at the University of California, San Francisco, have turned up evidence that we react to stimuli unconsciously before our conscious minds become involved.[9] Because intuition exists outside time, it can be thought of as the mediator of our relationship to the unknown, the vehicle for our being able to know before our conscious (i.e., left-brain) minds can record and process the knowing.

- Intuition as inner vision accessing the unconscious or supraconscious mind. To understand the meaning of this type of intuition we need to explain what we mean by *unconscious* and *supraconscious* mind.[10]

As noted in chapter 3, *mind* is not a physical entity in the brain. It has no physical location; it exists instead in a nonphysical, purely mental dimension that extends beyond the boundaries of the skin. It operates on the following four levels:

- Conscious mind. This is the level of logical consciousness with which we normally think and communicate. The level with which we are in touch while awake, this stratum of mind organizes daily life and serves to keep us alert and alive in the here and now. It is in direct contact with our senses and provides us with selective perception from a microscopic perspective as its attention is focused on one thing or another.
- Subconscious mind. The level just below the conscious mind, the subconscious is as active as the conscious mind but usually is not available to us. Whereas the conscious mind analyzes and uses logic, the subconscious mind synthesizes data, handles complexity, and recognizes the "big picture" through its holistic, macroscopic perspective. As a vast storehouse of visual, auditory, and sensory information, the subconscious mind holds great creative potential when accessed. Many techniques to stimulate creativity are designed to relax the conscious mind to gain access to this level. As we shall see in later chapters, intuitive imaging taps into this level of mind but also seems to reach two other layers—the unconscious and supraconscious levels of mind.
- Unconscious mind. The unconscious mind is beyond the subconscious mind, at a level even more basic and fundamental, a level where individual perceptions and memories interact with the outer world. This is the level of intuition and extrasensory perception, where "knowing" occurs be-

yond previous personal experience, via connections to other minds, events, or collective knowledge. The business person who "knows" not to take a flight that later crashes accesses this level of mind.

• Supraconscious mind—literally that aspect of mind that functions *above* the realm of normal consciousness. In our conception, however, the supraconscious is not merely above the conscious mind but is the larger field of awareness within which the conscious mind is more specifically focused, the vaster ocean of psychological reality within which our everyday consciousness swims. Sages, mystics, and people of wisdom throughout history have recognized and used this level of mind. Carl Jung called it the collective unconscious, the stratum that connects us to universal aspects of mind that provide direct knowing.[11] In that sense it represents a larger realm of principal ideas and knowledge fed by our collective consciousness, and out of which our everyday conscious awareness emerges.

In scientific terms, the supraconscious is the level of the "group field" about which we spoke in chapter 3 when we referred to Bell's theorem and Sheldrake's theory of the morphogenetic field. It also represents Bohm's "enfolded order," which is everywhere linked and out of which our physical reality unfolds. In this sense, it is the level of mind that forms the inner landscape for our physical world and the events in our lives.

Although the supraconscious mind is normally thought of as the domain of masters, sages, and holy men, it is not only these enlightened individuals that can tap into this level of awareness. It is an inherently human capability to link with the supraconscious mind and draw on its wisdom. This means that we all have within us the ability to access, under certain conditions, all the knowledge our human species has gained over the millennia. But how?

It is not as difficult as most of us might imagine. In fact, it may be as simple as relaxing the rational mind and engaging the imagination. In a famous example, Einstein used imagination and imagery to tap into the supraconscious realm of principal ideas. One night, while staring at the night sky, he used his imagination to ride a beam of light, almost as if he had become the light itself. The inner knowing that this imagery exercise produced led him to formulate his famous theory of relativity, which changed modern physics. Einstein later observed that *imagination is more powerful than knowledge.* For it is frequently our imagination that is the direct link with the supraconscious and the wisdom of the ages.

As we face the challenge of dealing with complexity and rapid change, we can draw on these levels of mind through the use of intuitive imaging. More and more people, in business and personal life, are doing just this—using their intuition and imaging ability to stay ahead of the curve—as attitudes about intuition are changing.

Changing Attitudes About Intuition

As discussed in chapter 3, our culture has been biased toward the left-brain logic and rationality that are part of scientism. Being neither quantifiable nor logical, intuition has often been denigrated as a "woman's thing," or as a lazy cop-out to avoid the rigorous analysis that "objective" science demands. Regrettably, we have been locked into a mindset that identifies left-brain logic and right-brain intuition as polar opposites. They aren't. And this either-or mentality keeps us from being as smart as we can be.

To open to our full potential, we must use our whole brain, not just half of it. For this to happen, we must first realize that intuition and reason are not opposites. They are complementary ways of knowing, as shown in Figure 4.1. What we have been taught is to value the externally driven, Newtonian way of knowing. In this "scientific" method, we engage our left-brain

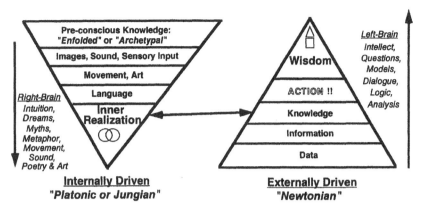

Figure 4.1   Knowledge Architectures

intellect to gather data, organize it into information, and process it through our experience to become knowledge (e.g., analyze, model, test, and validate it). Then through action, we apply what we learn. Over time, if we're lucky, we acquire wisdom. This is the guiding knowledge architecture for business, and most of our society. Yet there is another equally valid way of knowing that has been in use for millennia.

Eastern and aboriginal cultures have relied heavily on an inner process to know the world. Indeed, the perennial wisdom from all cultures has given right-brain knowing a place of honor from the earliest of times. This type of knowing can be viewed as Platonic or Jungian in nature. This is because "inner realization" flows from its source in the preconscious realm—what Plato called the "ideal plane," Jung called the "archetypal" or collective unconscious, what Bohm called the "enfolded" order, and what we have referred to as the supraconscious mind. In the scientific terms of holographic theory, it is a more fundamental "frequency domain" that is accessed through intuition and dreams, through images, sound, and sensory input. Insights can often be embodied or made conscious through movement and art and then distilled into language to give voice to the realization. It is an inner, subjective process that often happens in a flash. But this does not make it less valid than the externally driven, objective process. Moreover, to tap our expanded human potential and become as smart as we can be, we must learn to use our whole brain—right-brain intuition complementing left-brain reason in our quest to gain knowledge and understand the world. In fact, new science is moving us in this direction.

As new science produces more discoveries that invalidate the foundational principles of our dominant worldview (materialism, reductionism, determinism, and positivism), we are seeing a revision in thinking about the right brain and its intuition and nonrational modes of knowing. The societal and economic trends we noted in chapter 2 are fostering a rehabilitation of intuition. When the time frame for some decision making has been reduced to nanoseconds, disruptive change moves wholesale across the business landscape, and global competitive pressures intensify, it becomes essential to have a rapid, reliable, holistic way of knowing. As fast as the proverbial light bulb (which is an oft-used image for it), intuition is oriented to the future,[12] where all viable businesses now live. As more business people wake up to the reality that they too are living in the future, they are applying intuition in their lives and businesses.

Intuition at Work

Examples of how contemporary people are using intuition are so numerous that we must be selective. There is Marilyn Vos Savant, listed in the *Guinness Book of World Records* as having the highest IQ in the world, who regards intuition as an essential tool for problem solving.[13] Oliver Sachs, physician and author, uses his intuition all the time when making medical diagnoses.[14] Jonas Salk and Barbara McClintock, Nobel laureates both, were explicit about the value of intuition in their research.[15] John Brockman, a business executive involved in international sales, uses intuition as an interpretative tool to read between the lines of the garbled English translations of his foreign sales managers' reports.[16] Paul Fireman used his intuition when he decided to purchase the rights to an unknown British trademark called Reebok and make aerobic shoes[17]; in this case intuition was used to sense a trend before it became obvious. At the opening of her first cookie store, Debbie Fields acted on an intuition that told her to go out and sell her cookies on the streets[18]; the rest, as they say, is history. Jim Adamson, now the chief executive officer of Burger King, used his intuition when he was in the clothing business to overbuy a supply of imported jeans for the Gap clothing store[19]; the jeans sold out in less than thirty days. Dan Henslee, president of Hekman Furniture, Grand Rapids, Michigan, spotted the potential in the trend to home offices by means of his intuition.[20] Long before it was a recognized need, Henslee's company got into making desks for the home office and was able to sell five times the projections for this new line.

These individuals are not unusual. In a recent survey of business executives around the world conducted by the International Management Institute (IMI) in Geneva, fifty-four percent of business executives indicated that they use their intuition equally with logic to run their businesses.[21] Seventy-three percent of top managers rated themselves high or very high on intuition! They recognize that using intuition gives them a competitive edge and helps to keep them ahead of the curve.[22]

IMAGERY

Intuition is one component of intuitive imaging. The other is imagery. Whereas intuition is beyond conscious control, imagery is volitional. You can choose when, where, and how to use it. Like intuition, imagery has had changing fortunes in our culture and is gaining a better press as times change.

What do we mean when we speak of *imagery?* The English word *image* comes from the Latin *imago, imaginem,* through the Old French *imaginer,* meaning "to form a mental picture of."[23] The *Oxford English Dictionary* lists eighteen definitions for *image,* from statue and symbol, to simulation and copy.[24] For our purposes we define it as the "mental representation of something, not by direct perception, but by memory or imagination."[25] It is the natural language of mind and body. As the Latin root suggests, imaging is closely connected with imagination, and both words have had a checkered history in Western culture.

Changing Attitudes Toward Imagery

The power of images to affect reality has been known from the earliest of times. In some fashion, all cultures have worked with this power in their daily or religious lives. In the *I Ching*, a book that has been influential for three thousand years, we find that the ancient Chinese believed that "every event in the visible world is the effect of an image, that is, an idea in the unseen world."[26] The twelfth-century Persian Sufis agreed. They believed that in employing mental imagery one could "reshape the very fabric of one's destiny."[27] Sacred symbols and images have been used in ritual ceremony by priests and shamans of all cultures to intercede with Spirit to maintain harmony with the natural world, petition for rain, prepare for a hunt, ask for blessings, or travel shaman-like into altered states. Today even in our technological age, we still believe that certain religious images, symbols, or icons are invested with spiritual power and can even produce miracles. On a more mundane level, any ad agency worth its salt could write a treatise on the power of images in the media to promote brand identity, create a corporate or political image, or gain "share of mind" and thereby shape the buying preferences of modern-day shoppers.

Perhaps the power of images derives from the fact that they are more fundamental than language. Images are intimately connected with our belief structures and are a bridge between the physical world and the collective unconscious or supraconscious realm from which the physical world unfolds. As such the images we hold in our minds have great power to affect our everyday lives and businesses. Change what you hold in your mind and you change your reality. Emile Coué, a famous French psychotherapist of the early twentieth century, worked with autosuggestion—what we now might refer to as affirmations. He is famous for the affirmation, "Day by day, in every way, I am getting better and better." He found that, if people verbalized this statement and held it in their minds, they were able to significantly improve their lives. So powerful was this effect that he wrote, "When there is a conflict between the imagination and the will, the imagination always wins."[28] Indeed, reality is more malleable than we have been taught to believe. The images and associated beliefs that we hold most strongly in our minds are what we create in our lives. But if this is true, then why haven't we made greater use of the power that is available to us through mental imagery?

We mentioned in chapter 3 how the positivist, materialist bias of scientism has led to a tendency to disparage intangible, subjective things ("Oh, it's only your imagination!"). Imagery and imagination, in this paradigm, have been the stuff of childhood, with its imaginary playmates and things that go bump in the night. Throughout the first half of this century, most of the research into the power of mental imagery took place in Europe in the realm of psychology and psychosynthesis (e.g., Binet, Janet, Happich, Caslant, and Desoille). There was little or no research into imagery or imagination in the U.S., because of the stranglehold that scientism (and especially its psychological equivalent, called *behaviorism*)[29] had on our way of thinking. This began to change in the late 1960s, as cognitive psychologists and researchers in the field of artificial intelligence began to explore how we think.[30] In the 1970s and 1980s neuroscientists and brain researchers got into the act, so that by now imagery is recognized as an "integral part of how perception operates."[31] The hot new technology of medicine—positron-emission tomography (PET), computed tomography (CT), and magnetic resonance imaging (MRI)—puts imaging center stage, as computers produce medical scans or images of body parts that are then converted into pixels on a computer monitor to produce an image clinicians interpret to diagnose disease.[32]

Medicine is not the only area using imagery. We see great activity now in the computer software industry in regard to image processing.[33] Geneticists are exploring the genetics of imaging in the brain,[34] and imagery is being applied to improve daily life, health, sports performance, creativity, and business operations. As with intuition, because there are so many, we must be selective in citing examples of applications:

- To improve daily living, imagery is being used to lessen the anxiety associated with public speaking[35]; to stop children with chronic enuresis from wetting their beds[36]; to process anger,[37] to foster relaxation,[38] and to heal grief[39]; to counsel school students[40]; to facilitate fifth to eighth graders' learning of science[41]; and to improve problem-solving skills.[42]
- In the realm of health care, imaging techniques help smokers to quit,[43] and drug and alcohol addicts to break their habits.[44] When taught imagery techniques by nurses, patients heal faster and are able to leave the hospital sooner.[45] Imaging helps to control the pain of childbirth[46] and to manage anorexia.[47] It lessens both the incidence of infection after a surgical procedure[48] and the effects of chemotherapy[49] and helps to minimize hearing loss in noisy environments.[50]
- Athletic applications are among the most extensively documented, as noted in chapter 3. Regardless of whether it is an individual or team sport, virtually no sport has been immune to the influence of imaging—tennis,[51] golf,[52] archery,[53] figure skating,[54] basketball,[55] diving,[56] skiing,[57] lacrosse,[58] gymnastics,[59] football,[60] the high jump[61]—athletes in these sports have all benefited from the use of imagery, with improvements of sixty-one to ninety percent in some cases.[62]
- Imagery applied in the arts has sparked creativity.[63] It is used in architectural design and instruction[64] as well as in the plastic and performing arts. Scientific research on creativity and imaging indicates that imagers are more creative, sensitive, and adaptable to change.[65]
- To improve business performance. Business people are using imagery to create winning scenarios[66]; to change outmoded corporate and personal habits[67]; to improve the strategies of sales representatives[68]; to facilitate organiza-

tional development and change[69]; to solve problems faster and more accurately[70]; to foretell the future demise of competitors; to develop management strategies; to understand the deeper needs of employees; to break free of limited thinking patterns; to establish group vision or purpose; to set priorities; to discover latent customer needs (long before the customer recognizes them); to gain insights into relationship issues with customers, employees, and peers; and to plan personal futures within a company or industry.[71] With so many business applications, it is not surprising that imaging techniques are now being taught at leading U.S. business schools.[72]

We—the authors of this book—have done more than study imaging. We have used it for years in our own lives. Here are two stories illustrating how we have put the power of imagery to work for us.

John's Story

In the fall of 1983, I took the Silva Mind Method seminar. Working in the corporate world at the time and having an engineering background, I found the Silva Method to be very liberating. It gave me a direct experience of my natural intuitive abilities. It also reinforced for me the power of inner images to affect the outer world.

In holographic theory, a physical object and its image are mathematically interchangeable. The image exists in a more fundamental "frequency domain" from which the physical reality unfolds. This implies that the images we hold in our minds are as real as what we can reach out and touch. An image, held with intention and given enough energy, is, perhaps, just a more subtle form of the material world, a precursor to bringing it into being.

Theory aside, what I actually experienced in the Silva Method seminar is this: by using inner images we can actually program a result in our mind that affects our outer physical world. I discovered that imagery can achieve results that medical science could not.

My middle son, Sean, was six years old when I took the Silva Method course. He had warts on his hand that we had tried to eliminate for two years to no avail. Under the care of a family physician, we had them frozen off, burned off, and eaten away with acid. Each time they grew back. After I took the Silva course, I thought "Why not program them away using inner images?"

I taught Sean a simple Silva technique called the "Mind Mirror." First, he would see the problem, his warts, framed in a mirror of one color frame. This mirror he would smash. Then he would imagine his problem going away. For Sean, this entailed imagining little munchkins marching down into his warts with little picks, shovels, and dynamite, with which they would blow up the warts. When this was done, Sean would imagine the desired result—his hand free of warts in a mirror with a different color of frame.

Young kids are great. They don't know in advance that something can't be done, as adults often do. Sean performed this visualization each night before he went to sleep, believing that it would cure his condition. Six days later, he woke up with no warts on his hand! And they never returned.

Sue's Story

Six months after I went into business for myself I had a dream telling me that I would be buying a car in a very quick process that would leave me no time to shop around. Waking up, I recognized this as one of my "voice-over" dreams, a type of dream in which I am given explicit instructions. I had had such dreams for four years, and I knew they were always accurate. So I set to work, in my spare time, researching the type of car I would want to get. All this at a time when I barely had two cents to my name, but I knew from past experience that I had to trust the dream.

Once I had read *Consumer Reports* and other auto magazines, I had a list of cars to consider, and when the opportunity arose, I rented the Novas, Hondas, Mazdas, and Nissans that I had listed. Then I made up a very detailed visualization of my new car. I wanted a gray four-door Chevy Nova hatchback, with a light gray interior, automatic transmission, air conditioning, a stereo tape deck, and rear-window defroster. In my visualization I described the emotions and sensations I had when driving my new car— the thrill of the freedom it brought me, the pleasures of the air conditioning on a hot day, the joy of quadraphonic sound from the stereo. I read my visualization into a tape recorder and fell asleep each night for two weeks listening to my vivid image of a new car.

I did this for two weeks (not longer) because just as the dream indicated, I suddenly found myself with a very healthy income from a big project that left me no time at all to shop for a car. I found a car buyer, a man in the area who located cars for people and did the haggling with the salespeople, and I told him only that I wanted a small car along the lines of a Honda, Nova, Mazda, or Nissan with automatic transmission and air conditioning. I never told him all the particulars I had set down in my imagery, but I trusted that the imaging process would bring me exactly what I had envisioned. So it was. Mr. Price (the car buyer) called me less than 24 hours after I had initially called him to report that he had found me a gray Chevy Nova hatchback with lots of extras. It not only had all that I had imagined, it had more—power locks, carpet covers, additional mirrors. It was another proof of the power of imaging to create reality.

KEY FEATURES OF IMAGING

What are business school students, nurses, coaches, or home-makers doing when they practice imaging? There are many techniques and "schools" of imaging, but they share certain features.

The first is to get clear on the goal. What is it that you want to bring about? What is the question? What do you want to change?

The second feature is relaxation. All imaging processes employ relaxation as the way to allow the normally subordinate right brain to come to the fore while the conscious mind recedes.

The third feature varies depending on the type and purpose of the imagery. In health care and sports applications, an image is often developed in conjunction with the doctor, nurse, or trainer to achieve the goal. The image is developed first and then focused on. In business, creativity, and general applications, the imagination is allowed to produce images spontaneously.

The fourth element common to all forms of imaging is the interpretation of the results. In sports and health, there is evaluation of the physical result—better health or a more accurate golf swing. In business and creativity, the image must be decoded or related to the stated goal or question.

There are other elements of imagery unique to specific types of imaging. We explore one particularly powerful type—intuitive imaging—in chapter 5.

NOTES

1. *Webster's Third International Dictionary*, 1187.
2. Vaughn 1979, 98.
3. Agor 1986, 5.
4. Vaughn 1979, 66–7.
5. Ibid., 69–70.
6. Cf. von Franz and Hillman 1971; Keirsey and Bates 1984.
7. Keirsey and Bates 1984, 25.
8. Nadel, Haims, and Stempson 1989, 2.
9. Libet 1980; 1985; 1987.

10. Parikh 1994, 33–4.
11. Hopcke 1989, 14–5.
12. Keirsey and Bates 1984, 18–9.
13. Nadel, Haims, and Stempson 1989, 1.
14. Ibid., 3.
15. Cf. ibid., 7; Keller 1983, 198, 200–4.
16. Emery 1995, 41.
17. Ibid.
18. Ibid., 42.
19. Ibid.
20. Ibid.
21. Parikh 1994, 63.
22. Ibid., 55.
23. *Oxford English Dictionary*, VII, 665.
24. Ibid., 665–7.
25. Ibid., 666.
26. Wilhelm and Baynes 1967, lvii.
27. Talbot 1991, 260.
28. Fanning 1988, preface.
29. Hilgard 1981, 5–66.
30. Kosslyn 1994, 2.
31. Ibid., 21.
32. *Random House Unabridged Dictionary*, 955.
33. *Reader's Guide to Periodical Literature* May 1995, 355.
34. Kosslyn 1994, 407.
35. Senqi 1992, 1067–73.
36. Butler 1993, 215–7.
37. Slomine 1993, 671–6.
38. *Good Morning America* 1996, 21.
39. Creen 1992.
40. Myrick and Myrick 1993, 62–70.
41. Konopak 1991, 309–19.
42. Antonietti 1991, 211–27.
43. Wynd 1992, 184–9, 196.
44. Ahsen 1993, 1–60.
45. Rancour 1991, 30–3.
46. Korol and von Baeyer 1992, 167–72.
47. Luzzato 1994, 139–43.
48. This has been demonstrated by Jerry Whitworth, surgeon at Columbia Presbyterian Hospital, New York; *ABC Evening News* 1996.
49. Troesch 1994, 7–8.
50. Munson 1995, 24.
51. Suinn 1983, 514–5.
52. Ibid.; cf. Murphy 1992, 444; and Betts 1995, 48–9.
53. Deschaumes-Molinari 1991, 29–36.

54. Palmer 1992, 148–55.
55. Savoy 1993, 173–90.
56. Grouios 1992, 60–9.
57. Suinn 1983, 514–5.
58. Brewer and Shillinglaw 1992, 139–47.
59. Liggett and Hamada 1993, 190–7.
60. Suinn 1983, 514–5.
61. Ibid.
62. Ibid., 515.
63. Lindauer 1983, 472–500.
64. Downing 1992, 441–70.
65. Richardson 1983, 35–6.
66. McGarvey 1992, 126.
67. Neck and Manz 1992, 681.
68. Neumeier 1990, 34.
69. Weaver and Cotrell 1991, 91; Howe 1989, 70.
70. Antonietti 1991, 211–27.
71. These have been ways we have personally used imaging in our business ca-
    reers. We provide explicit examples of these usages in later chapters.
72. Ray and Myers 1986, 69, 72.

Intuitive Imagery

5

> Unless there is a gigantic conspiracy involving . . . highly respected scientists in various field, many of them originally hostile to the claims of the psychic researchers, the only conclusion the unbiased observer can come to must be that there are people who obtain knowledge existing in other people's minds, or in the outer world, by means yet unknown to science.
>
> *Professor H.J. Eysenck*

Intuitive imaging is a powerful form of imagery that has several special features not found in most other imaging techniques. In this chapter we identify what intuitive imagery is, how it works and differs from other forms, and how it has been used in real-life application. In subsequent chapters we lead you through the steps and give advice about how to formulate the questions and interpret the images that result.

WHAT IS INTUITIVE IMAGERY?

Intuitive imagery is a time-tested, whole-brain process that harnesses intuition in a reliable, disciplined way. It works by bypassing the dominant left brain and its rationality to allow the intuitive right brain to "speak" through images and feelings. Because these images come from deeper levels of consciousness, they are able to transcend emotional attachments, fears, anxieties, and "mind funnels" (habits of perception) that limit what we see and know. Once the right brain has been allowed to speak through images and feelings, the left brain is re-engaged to interpret, validate, and apply the information received.

As shown in Figure 5.1, intuitive imaging is a balanced, whole-brain process. The right brain taps our inner knowing to see into the future and produce vision while the left brain designs the imaging exercises, provides focus, and deals with application. Both hemispheres draw upon their individual strengths. Although it seems obvious, we frequently forget that both are necessary to realizing our full human potential.

Intuitive imaging is an outgrowth of guided imaging processes that have all had a common goal: to gain access to knowledge that the conscious, rational mind alone could not provide. Its roots go back to ancient times. Although it is done in a waking state, intuitive imaging shares a similarity to dream incubation techniques that were common in ancient Egypt, Greece, China, India, and in early Christian and Islamic practices.[1] In fact, early work with guided imagery techniques were called "waking dreams" (Desoille in France), "guided reverie" (Guillerey in

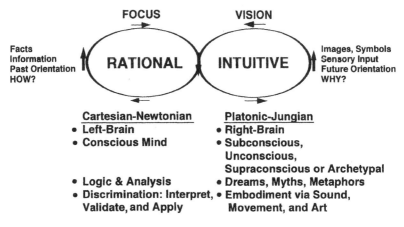

Figure 5.1 Whole-Brain Knowing

Switzerland), or "dream therapy" (Virel and Frétigny's "onirotherapie").[2] In its use of guide questions, intuitive imaging is similar to many guided imagery processes used in psychotherapy and psychosynthesis starting with pioneering work by Janet at the turn of the century. In its use of transformational symbols, it is similar to early work by Happich, Caslant, and others. What is different about intuitive imagery is its pragmatic focus. It is a process that can be used to harness deep levels of inner knowing to produce practical information and insight for use in business and daily life—sometimes with spectacular results.

Intuitive imaging has evolved from a process developed by Magaly Rodriguez, initially called "light imagery work" and later "creative imagery." Although her conclusions were implicit in much earlier work in guided imagery, Rodriguez recognized that intentions held in the mind of the guide were somehow received by the person doing the actual imaging. This communication between guide and imager is nonverbal. It takes place mentally on an intuitive level. Rodriguez began to make use of this understanding to intentionally bypass the rational mind and evoke images that produced deeper levels of knowing and insight. In her early work, Rodriguez actually considered creative imagery to be a form of waking meditation, or guided visual prayer, with the power to communicate at the "soul level." In our ten years of using imagery techniques in both business and personal applications, we agree with Rodriguez on the depth of communication and insight available by using intuitive imagery. We share her passion for expanding its use in the business arena.

For all its depth and power, intuitive imagery is easy to learn, is usable anywhere, and requires no special skills or "gifts." Anyone can do it, and it is effective in a wide array of contexts and over wide distances. Participants can be separated by thousands of miles and the process still produces valid answers. It yields not only answers but also awe when people use it for the first time and discover their vast personal potential for accessing their inner wisdom.

THE ELEMENTS OF INTUITIVE IMAGING

How do ordinary people acquire an "open sesame" to their su-praconscious mind? As noted in chapter 4, intuitive imagery is an imagery method that shares features common to all forms of imagery work. These are as follows:

- Defining the goal. What do you want to address? What area of life or particular problem do you want insight about? If you are like most people, you have many concerns and lots of questions to which you'd like answers. If so, you need to list each concern separately and perform the intuitive imaging process for one question at a time.
- Relaxing. This is a way to encourage the emergence of the right brain. Close your eyes. Center yourself, and consider yourself taking a journey into the realm of your imagination.
- Observing the images. In the intuitive imagery process (unlike in sports or health imaging techniques) images are allowed to come spontaneously. Be a passive observer. Don't censor, judge, or try to interpret what comes to you; just watch and describe. This description can be written or oral (shared with someone else, if you are working with a partner, or spoken into a tape recorder).
- Interpreting the results. How do the images you received relate to the question you had? This last element may seem straightforward, but it is not, because intuitive imagery has an additional feature not found with most other imaging techniques—the blind process, or intuitive key. When you use the imaging process, you do not know the question for which you are receiving images.

This blind nature of imaging is a key feature of intuitive imagery because this is how the process bypasses the rational mind. If you choose a question of importance to you, it is likely that you have thought about it beforehand. Your left-brain logic and rationality have been brought to bear on the issue, and along with your logic you bring unconscious habits of perception, mental ruts, or blocks—all of which can contaminate the process, limit innovation, or impede finding a solution. Intuitive imagery gets around this by allowing the creativity, innovation, and open-mindedness of the right brain to provide another perspective.

We call this blind process using *intuitive keys,* because they are used to access your intuitive knowing while bypassing your ego-mind. You get images that address your concerns but without your rational mind's knowing which images represent what issues until the process is over and the keys are revealed. The way this works is this: If you are performing intuitive imagery with someone else, you write your questions and then, while holding these questions in your mind, have your partner come up with images, but without any knowledge of what your real question is. If you are doing intuitive imagery alone, first you write several questions on index cards (one per card). Then turn them over, shuffle them until you no longer know which card has which question and then number the cards, face down. Next, get images for each, record these images, and only then do you turn up the cards to reveal what the questions were. (See chapter 7 for detailed guidelines.)

By now, your rational mind is probably wondering how you can get valid images without knowing the question. This is possible because you are really posing your question on two levels. There is the prompt on the verbal level, called a *guide* question, when you ask your partner (or yourself) for an image, for example, "Go to a place," or "See a door." But simultaneously you are silently giving the hidden, unknown instruction to which your intuitive right brain responds. When the right brain hears "Go to a place," it produces images of a place that represent the answer to your original question.

Here's an example of the use of the intuitive key. Let's say you want to know how your business looks at the moment. You write this question on a piece of paper, but you don't reveal it to your partner. Instead you prompt your partner with "Go to a place, look around and tell me what you see." Your partner receives an image and reports, "I see a ship on a stormy ocean being tossed around and unable to hold a course." Your partner has had no clue what your *real* question was, but nonetheless is able to provide an image related to your concern. How is this possible?

HOW INTUITIVE IMAGERY WORKS

In chapter 3 we presented some of the science that explains how intuitive imagery works—how electromagnetic and morphogenetic fields interpenetrate everything in the universe outside the bounds of time and space; how our minds are all linked, in the interconnectedness and nonlocality of Bell's theorem; how time is relative in the Einsteinian universe, making possible our tapping into the future; how in holographic theory the coherence produced by mental relaxation and the prompts of the intuitive imagery process can produce access to universal mind; how the mind functions on levels, including that of the Collective Unconscious, with its archetypes that contain all the wisdom of human history. All these discoveries explain how it is that you can pose a question without sharing it openly with someone else and then have relevant, meaningful images come from that person's mind.

In summary, there is an accumulating array of experimental evidence that proves that we can tap into the minds of others to send and receive thoughts and images. It seems to be a natural human ability. Moreover, reality appears to be a "living hologram"[3] of which we are each individual, interconnected parts. Remember, a unique aspect of the hologram is that each part has access to the whole. So we, as individual parts of the universal hologram, have access to all the knowledge stored or *enfolded* in it, including knowledge of objects, people, and the accumulated wisdom of the ages.

To bring this back to why intuitive imagery works, consider this: The thoughts you have as you pose your question are a form of energy and information that can be communicated, directed, and received by the mind of another person. Thoughts are actually things that we send out that affect the world around us. Just as the scientific subjects in Robert Jahn's laboratory affected the results of the random event generating machine, so you can affect the images that appear in your partner's mind. All of us, as human beings, are far *more* sensitive receivers of thought energy than any machine. We can pick up and process far richer information, with our right brain, than any computer can. Operating on the premise that people can and do communicate mentally through images, the natural language of the mind, intuitive imagery takes advantage of our vast human potential and harnesses it for practical use.

At this point you might wonder if this is ethical. If our minds can pick up all sorts of information in the intuitive imagery process, can it invade our personal privacy? Does it give insights into me that I don't want to reveal? When we demonstrate intuitive imagery in workshops, there are always people concerned about the ethical dimension. Our response is twofold. First, we emphasize when we teach intuitive imagery that the process should be used only with the permission of the participant. Second, we have seen from experience that when a participant does not wish to share, the images received by the partner either disappear, are vague, or are not interpretable. We seem to have a built-in unconscious defense mechanism that operates for our highest good and protection, assuring our privacy. Table 5.1 presents the ethical dos and don'ts of intuitive imagery.

If all of the foregoing sounds bizarre or unbelievable, remember that your normal consciousness, rooted in the left brain, operates in a logical, linear manner and functions as a "voice of judgment,"[4] that tries to block novel ways of thinking and living. The left brain does not want to believe in what it cannot verify with the five physical senses. As noted at the end of chapter 3, however, you will never see it with your eyes until you first believe it. You may need to consciously suspend a critical inner voice that insists the intuitive imagery process is impossible. At the outset you need to be open to accommodating a new experience and withholding judgment until you try the process yourself. Give it a fair test and *then* decide. After teaching intuitive imagery to thousands of people, we know from empirical results that it *does* work.

Table 5.1 Ethical Dos and Don'ts of Intuitive Imaging

Do	*Don't*
Use intuitive imagery with an explicit set of ethical standards	Use intuitive imagery as a tool to exploit or manipulate or for personal gain at the expense of others
Use intuitive imagery with a high purpose and clear intention to achieve positive results	Use intuitive imagery without grounding or in the absence of the rational mind as a check
Use intuitive imagery to facilitate personal introspection, growth, and healing	Use intuitive imagery for ego gratification
Use intuitive imagery to cultivate deeper sensitivity for people, circumstances, and events	Use intuitive imagery superficially, without taking steps to deepen understanding
Use intuitive imagery to foster change on both personal and organizational levels	Use inappropriately the energy that intuitive imagery makes available, such as in a way that causes divisiveness or fear
Use intuitive imagery to help create a sense of connectedness among people	Use intuitive imagery to *force* growth or transformation
Use intuitive imagery with a commitment to seeking the highest good for all concerned	Use intuitive imagery in a way that is invasive of or disregards the privacy of others

RESULTS AND BENEFITS OF USING INTUITIVE IMAGERY

More than just "work," intuitive imagery has provided a rich array of benefits, personal and professional, in the lives of the people who have used it. In the personal realm, we have seen intuitive imagery promote self-trust, strengthen individuals' concepts of themselves, and enhance creativity by allowing people to tap into their inner genius. Like meditation, intuitive imagery is health-giving. To those who are sick—or like John's son Sean with his warts, suffering from an unpleasant physical condition—intuitive imagery speeds healing. To those in good health, it provides increased energy. Because it works at the soul level, the level of supraconscious mind, intuitive imagery causes deep, fundamental changes in people that enrich their spiritual life. As noted earlier, after our workshops it is not uncommon for participants to report feelings of awe, wonder, and empowerment at the discovery of their inner wisdom.

In professional life, many men and women in business have used intuitive imagery to verify hunches, to streamline the decision-making process, and to increase performance and accelerate learning. Intuitive imagery affords managers an objective view of the problems and potentials of their business, increasing the likelihood of sound judgment calls and overall success. When planning for the future, managers have used intuitive imagery to obtain information about the probable outcomes of different courses of action, enabling changes in strategy and tactics that make the business more viable and boost the bottom line. Intuitive imagery also has promoted cohesive, effective teamwork and the development of shared visions and has helped to foster a spirit of community among employees and managers. Table 5.2 summarizes the business circumstances in which intuitive imagery is most valuable.

Consider the following real-life examples of how intuitive imagery has been put to good use (see chapters 10 and 11 for dozens of others):

> *Beating the competition through imaging.* Bill, one of the members of the SWAT (special weapons and tactics) team we formed inside DuPont, had a daughter, Lisa, who was a very talented ice skater. She was eleven years old in 1989 and getting ready to compete for the U.S. Junior National Championship. Earlier that year, the SWAT team had begun to work with imagery to harness the power of the intuitive mind. Once exposed to the process, Bill decided to

Table 5.2 Business Circumstances in Which Intuitive Imagery Is Most Valuable

Organizational	*Personal*
Providing insight into personnel development needs and checking assignment fit	Finding or clarifying life purpose, creating a personal vision, and discovering personal gifts
Discovering the latent needs of customers, clients, or patients	Improving the quality of relationships and resolving interpersonal issues
Prioritizing and allocating efforts and resources; reviewing budgets	Making choices and prioritizing efforts
Evaluating research and development and marketing options and generating new options and alternatives	Anticipating and discovering the probable outcomes of decisions and identifying paths around potential barriers
Discovering and prioritizing market needs	Testing perceptions and different approaches to issues
Business forecasting, evaluating strategies, reviewing business ideas or hunches	Discovering the nature of underlying problems before they fully surface
Designing events, preparing travel agendas or important meetings	Reducing or removing the obstacles to greater success, such as confusion, fear, or anxiety
Optimizing organizational structure and work flow	Identifying and removing blocks to productivity and creativity
Preparing presentations, materials, and speeches	Verifying hunches and promoting self-confidence

use it with Lisa, because she was having trouble with her triple jumps. Bill and Lisa began to use imagery to perfect the jumps in her mind, much as Jack Nicklaus did in his golf game (as described in chapter 3). The more Lisa practiced the jumps in her mind, the better, more confident, and relaxed she became. In the 1990 competition, she placed second in the junior nationals.

Finding a new job. A friend of mine, introduced to intuitive imagery in a *Fortune* 500 company, uses it almost daily. He has worked with it over the past seven years in both his business and personal lives, building his confidence in its usefulness and accuracy. Jerry[5] left the corporate world in 1991 to travel and create his own small training business. He and his wife, Jean, became experts at personal transformation processes and cultivated a diverse clientele across the country. More and more, however, they found they wanted to live a quiet, simple life close to the earth with lots of breathing space and a steady income. After selling most of what they owned and traveling almost constantly for more than three years, settling down was a big change. Yet it seemed to be right. They decided to look for an employer who could meet three criteria. First, they did not want to have to buy or rent a house. Second, they wanted to work only twenty to twenty-five hours per week. Third, they wanted to work together. With this image of the ideal job in mind, they began to search for potential employers, finding ten that might fit the specifications. One, an entrepreneur, stood out from the rest in terms of benefits and location, offering lodging, a modest salary, and a future house of their choosing. Jerry and Jean decided to go all out for it. Intuitive imagery was their ally in achieving their objective.

After contacting the prospective employer and finding out basic information, Jerry and Jean used imaging at each step of the decision process to decide among alternative approaches, confirm the timing of letters and phone calls, gain insight into the interview process, and quantify their salary request. The particular intuitive imagery technique they used consisted of opening a series of doors and rating feelings and images received. Jerry asked the imaging questions, and Jean got the impressions. The intensity of Jean's feelings tapped accurately into the energy of the alternatives.

It is important to note, in this story, that there was an element of time pressure to this process: Making a commitment to settle in for the winter meant turning down other opportunities. Jerry and Jean needed a place to stay soon. Rationally neither of them knew whether the new job would pan out. But the intuitive imagery process, which they had learned to trust over time, told them to stay the course. They had confidence in the deeper insight they were getting, and they were not disappointed: Based on the intuitive imagery, Jerry and Jean got a luncheon interview, asked for the high end of their desired salary range, and were hired the same day. Every one of their criteria were met—lodging, part-time work, and working together. They later found out that this entrepreneur had 150 applications for the job, but conducted only one interview—theirs!

Like Bill, Lisa, Jerry, and Jean, you can use intuitive imagery to find a home, negotiate a raise, get insight into your purpose in life, plan your retirement, or develop a business strategy. The applications are limited only by your imagination. To find out how to make intuitive imagery work for you, turn to the step-by-step instructions and guidelines we provide in Part III.

NOTES

1. Crampton, An Historical Survey of Mental Imagery Techniques in Psychotherapy and Description of the Dialogic Imagery Method. Self-published, undated, p. 1.
2. Ibid., p. 11.
3. Talbot 1991, 145.
4. This phrase was coined by the students in Michael Ray's Creativity in Business course at Stanford University; Ray and Myers 1986, 40.
5. The names of the individuals in this story have been changed.

III

How to Use Intuitive Imagery

6

Intuitive Imaging Formula

The imagination is more powerful than knowledge.

Albert Einstein

In this chapter we describe the six steps involved in intuitive imaging. Illustrations and exercises are provided to help you understand the process and how to work with it. Figure 6.1 presents the six steps.

STEP 1: DEFINING THE PROBLEM

This step may seem simple or obvious, but there are some important points to keep in mind to obtain good results with the process. Doing intuitive imaging is rather like working with a computer: garbage in, garbage out. If your initial question is vague, general, or fuzzy, you won't get much more than vague, general, or fuzzy answers. A quality question is the first step in receiving a quality answer.

Be sure your question is a simple, not a compound, question. A compound question is one to which more than one answer is required. For example, "Should I go to Phoenix for the sales meeting?" is a single question. "Should I go to Atlanta for

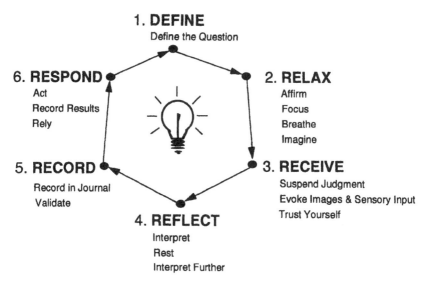

Figure 6.1 The Imaging-Reflection-Response Cycle

the sales meeting and meet Bob there to discuss the new market strategy?" is a compound question. Break compound questions into their separate parts and perform imagery on the individual parts.

When you are at a beginner's stage of working with intuitive imagery, it is best to start with simple, meaningful, and specific questions. The simplest are questions that can be answered *yes* or *no*. Images with this type of question are simpler to interpret than those with other questions, as is explained in chapter 8.

We suggest that the questions you pose in doing intuitive imagery be meaningful, that is, important to you. This is because the imagery process works by picking up the energy and intent linked to the question by the person asking it. If the question is trivial or frivolous, it is not invested with much energy, and the resulting images are usually vague, poor, or difficult to interpret.

Be specific in formulating your question. Focus on a single, clear objective, such as "What is the market going to be in the next six months for our new line of carpet products?" Specificity makes the imaging results easier to deal with, especially if you are just beginning to use the process. This is not to suggest that you must always pose specific questions. As you become more familiar and comfortable with the intuitive imagery process, you can pose general questions to receive rich images and provide a general overview of a situation. Such general questions, and the imagery results, are often exactly what is needed, especially in the early stages of a new organization, or when a new product is coming on line. General questions are also great for generating new ideas and information, when not all the facts are in. Asking for a general overview with a general question often produces new and unexpected information, which is useful for expanding your thinking and planning ability.

A final component of defining the question is being clear about what you really want. None of the steps yields results if you really are not open to receiving an answer. This is because your right-brain intuitive side is aware of unconscious psychological defenses and blocks answers that it knows you do not want to hear. Asking a question you are not ready to have answered usually results in no images, or images that are vague or cannot be interpreted.

STEP 2: RELAX AND PREPARE YOURSELF

As noted in earlier chapters, relaxation and preparation are features of all imaging techniques, because they allow the right brain to come out of the shadow of the dominant left brain. On the face of it, relaxing seems simple, but in the ten years of experience we have had teaching intuitive imagery to thousands of people, we have discovered that relaxation is not easy for many people. So here, and in several appendices, we provide some relaxation techniques.[1] You might try them all and choose the one that works best for you.

Basic to all four techniques are making yourself comfortable and giving the process adequate time. Loosen your clothing, such as collars, belts, anything tight. Go to the bathroom before beginning the process. Ensure that you will not be distracted: unplug the phone or turn on your voice mail; go into a quiet room, if necessary. Plan to commit at least a half hour; don't try to rush through the steps. If you are doing the process at home, you might lie down. Set your intention to become relaxed. Then assume whatever posture and facial expression you would have if you *were* very relaxed. Feel what it feels like to be very relaxed. Breathe as you would if you were very relaxed. Think what you would think if you were very relaxed. If you do all these things, you *will* enter a relaxed state.[2]

Relaxation Technique 1: Clearing Your Body of Stress

Most of us carry nervous tension in our neck and shoulders as well as other areas of our bodies. Clearing away this tension enhances one's ability to receive clear images. Try the head and neck exercises and the progressive muscle tension and relaxation exercises in Appendix 2. Then close your eyes. Let your eyes close gently without forcing them shut. Let your eyeballs rotate slightly upward (about fifteen to twenty degrees) and inward, so that you are looking at the center of your forehead. When the eyes are rotated in this manner, there is an increase in alpha brain waves,[3] which are linked to feelings of well-being, heightened awareness, and creativity. Even though helpful, this eye rotation is not essential to effective imaging. Nothing is absolutely required, not even closing your eyes. Some people receive better images with their eyes open. The cardinal rule is do what feels right for you. Experiment and find what works best.

Finally, *allow* yourself to relax. This is the most important factor. Simple relaxation does the most to enhance the quality of your imaging. In a normal state of awareness, the brain produces a predominance of beta waves (more than 14 hertz). When you are relaxed, the brain produces alpha brain waves (7 to 14 hertz), which enhance your ability to visualize and receive clear images.

Relaxation Technique 2:
Focusing Your Mind

In our normal waking awareness, many of us spend our time any place but in the present moment. We think about the past and wish things had been different. We worry about what the future holds. The past or the future is not where our power lies. We form our lives from our focal point in the present. Learning to focus is about being present *right now*, in *this* moment. Cultivating the ability to focus totally on the present moment has at least two benefits. First, you will be able to receive images that are clearer and uncontaminated by concerns over the past or worries about the future. Second, you will gain more power in your life. For practical purposes, focusing is one of the most important concepts in the imaging formula.

The principle behind focusing is to help you quiet the mind talk that keeps you from being in the *now*. When you focus and become centered in the present moment, your mind is more receptive to your inner images. There are several ways to quiet your talkative, logical mind so you can better focus on the inner images and symbols presented by your intuitive mind. These include the following:

- Focusing on a sound, such as instrumental music
- Focusing on a phrase or mantra
- Focusing visually on an object, shape, or picture
- Focusing the senses on the here and now to experience being totally present

In Appendix 2, we provide exercises you can try for each one of these types of focus.

Relaxation Technique 3:
Breathing

Babies breathe in a natural way that activates both hemispheres of the brain. If you watch a sleeping baby breathe, you will notice a natural rhythmic pattern. First the upper chest inflates. Then the breath pushes out the diaphragm in the belly area. The belly area deflates. Then the chest area recedes. Many of us have forgotten how to breathe naturally like this; our breathing is shallow, primarily into the upper chest. This shallow breathing activates the left hemisphere of the brain, which controls logic and organization. Breathing deeper into the belly activates the right hemisphere and the limbic system, which enhances feelings, creativity, and envisioning capabilities. Breathing deeper into the belly is desirable as a preparation for receiving clear images. In Appendix 2, we present six breathing exercises you might try.

Relaxation Technique 4:
Relaxing Through Imagining

You can use your imagination to help you relax. It is simple yet powerful. In this technique, you imagine yourself to be anywhere you desire, anywhere that is particularly peaceful, relaxing, or blissful. Because the subconscious mind does not differentiate between objective reality "out there" and your internal imaging reality, your body responds to what you imagine. This is the reason why visualization works to prepare athletes for peak performance and why cancer patients work with internal images to strengthen their immune systems. Using the same powerful imagining technique, you can relax your body and become more receptive to your intuition. We offer three guided visualizations in Appendix 2.

The final component of Step 2 is preparing yourself by use of affirmations. Affirmations are strong, positive, feeling-rich statements about having already achieved a desired result. They can be powerful aids to opening to your intuition and receiving clear images. It is important that affirmations be in the present tense and written in the positive rather than the negative. Affirmations are especially powerful when spoken aloud and combined with clear, vivid, positive visualizations. They work by reprogramming the subconscious mind, which does not have the same sense of linear or sequential time as the conscious mind. Affirmations replace negative self-talk, help you to suspend judgment, and set doubts aside. Your subconscious mind interprets these positive statements and visualizations as *already accomplished* and therefore becomes a powerful ally in eliminating barriers to reaching your goal.

In Appendix 2 we provide some affirmations that can be used to strengthen your intuitive ability. Choose one that feels right for you, or write your own. Say the affirmation aloud. At the same time, visualize yourself achieving the result to create an internal experience of success. Make the image vivid. Repeat this often. Post the affirmation on the refrigerator. Keep it in your awareness. Remember, you are sending a message to your subconscious that the desired result has already been achieved. What you affirm and visualize consistently can easily become a reality. Affirmations work!

STEP 3: RECEIVE IMAGES

Practicing the exercises in Step 2 brings you physiological and psychological benefits. However, our primary purpose for practicing relaxation and centering techniques is to enter a receptive state where we allow our inner images to flow freely. This free flow of visual and sensory images is enhanced greatly by experiencing a real connection to our higher intuitive guidance, higher self, our soul, or the higher forces of the universe. Whatever name you have for it, we become more receptive to our inner genius when we open to a higher power and actually feel that connection. When this happens, we are more likely to suspend judgment, receive images, and trust the information we obtain.

Linking with a Higher Power   The following guided visualization[4] is designed to teach you to find your mental screen and improve your ability to receive images. You might want to read it into a tape recorder and play it back to yourself frequently in the early stages of your imaging work. It will help you become more grounded and balanced. At the same time, it will also help you feel more connected to inner guidance from your higher self and to feel a stronger link with a higher power. It needs only a few minutes to do, yet every time you do it, you make each subsequent connection stronger and easier.

1. Close your eyes and relax. Allow your breathing to become deeper, fuller, and very relaxed. Take several slow breaths, breathing down into your belly and expanding your entire chest. As you inhale, imagine you are breathing in golden particles of light that travel throughout your body to cleanse and wash away tension or anxiety. As you exhale, let go of any worries, cares, or concerns, any thoughts of activities or things that you have to get done, and say to yourself, "relax."

2. With your eyelids still closed, let your eyes roll gently upward and inward, focusing on a point in the center of your forehead. Now relax your eyes slightly. The area you see in your mind just beyond your forehead is your mental screen where your inner images will appear. Imagine the screen to be black at first, the color of calling things into being. As you focus on this screen with intent, you will be able to access your inner knowing. As you project images from your external reality onto this screen, you will be able to make changes in your images, yourself, and your life.

3. On your mental screen, see your favorite place in nature, a place that you find safe and nurturing. Now project yourself into this image. Begin to feel your connection to the earth and to all life on it. Stretch out your feelings to become the earth beneath your feet, the grass and the trees, the breeze that rustles through your leaves, the cool rocks and clear streams, the dark ocean depths, the many different animals, and all people everywhere. You are simultaneously rooted in the earth and free to travel wherever your inner senses carry you. Experience yourself as the elements: earth, water, fire, and air. Expand your awareness to feel your joyful connection to the creative energy of life itself, to the Earth Mother, to the womb of all life. Drink in its energy until

it fills every cell of your body with the renewing power of creation.

4. Bring your awareness back to your body, to your center just below your navel. Begin to radiate this new earth energy outward and around you, forming a luminous egg of protection from any negative or detrimental influences.

5. Now you are grounded and ready to connect with the higher planes of reality. Move your awareness to the top of your head and experience an opening of the energy center there in the crown. You may feel a tingling sensation as this begins to happen, or a ring of energy begin to form around your head creating a slight pressure at the temples and the back of the head. As you open this crown chakra, visualize a beam of light going out from the top of your head and extending straight up as far as you can imagine.

6. Imagine you are connecting with a higher power—with your higher self, with your spirit guides, with the elders or ascended masters, with the angelic realm, or with the God-force and creator of all life. Connect with the highest energy that you are able to receive at this time. Let your body soak in this energy, into every cell and synapse. Feel your vibrations being raised.

7. Imagine that your mind is now linked to the universal mind, the All-That-Is, that your thoughts now clearly reflect the higher planes of reality. Picture your will becoming one with the higher will, as a cord of light extends from the area of your solar plexus, in the center of your chest just below your breast bone, and linking with the source of all life. Each time you imagine this link, and the more strongly you can feel it, you are making it real for you.

8. It is time to connect with your soul or Higher Self. Visualize your soul as a clear blue flame starting at the top of your head and expanding to envelop your entire body. Feel the energy of your soul bathing you in its cool radiance. Allow yourself to become one with it and ask for a deeper, more conscious connection. Sincere requests are always heard. Your Higher Self will respond and immediately begin helping you strengthen your connection to its guidance and direction.

9. Now bring your awareness and attention back to the top of your head. This is where telepathic communication from the higher dimensions occurs. Your imagination is like a powerful satellite dish antenna that can receive any broadcast that you desire, simply by your intending it to do so. All you need to establish the link is to use the power of your imagination to mentally adjust your receiver to tune into the broadcast. As you strengthen this telepathic connection, the images that you receive become aligned with your highest purpose and that of all others.

10. As you begin to receive images on your mental screen, remember to suspend judgment and trust yourself. Allow the images that come to you to be OK. Don't judge them or try to figure out what they mean. Release preconceived ideas. Be open to new information. Expect the unexpected. Everything you receive comes from some part of you. Trust whatever comes into your mind, without editing or making it wrong. Remember that your first image or intuitive response is often the clearest.

STEP 4: REFLECTING ON AND INTERPRETING IMAGES

Only in this step does the left brain join the process. Because this step of interpretation is both complex and central to making intuitive imagery useful, we devote an entire chapter, chapter 8, to it. Here we only delineate the general process and components involved in interpreting images.

You have, by this point, worked with the intuitive imagery process and have received images. As noted in chapter 4, images are the natural language of the mind and body. Given the verbal, left-brain bias of our culture, we usually do not realize this: words are not naturally how our bodies "speak." Words are merely left-brain symbolic representations of images. Images are more fundamental. Young children think by means of images, and the soul speaks by means of images, as the perspicacious psychologists (lit. *students of the soul*) admit. Our dreams are eloquent every night in producing multiple images. The key to accessing the wisdom of our dreams and imagery is learning to decode the language they speak.

Images can be more than visual. They can come as physical feelings or auditory stimuli. When you are learning to work with images, you need to be open to the full range of bodily sensations. Eventually you will come to recognize your most natural and usual forms of imaging.

Another key component in interpreting imagery is being open. You must be willing to accept what an image is saying—its meaning—even if it threatens current beliefs or attitudes. Intuitive imagery, as a process, cuts through perceptual filters to go to the core of your concerns. The result is that sometimes you get images that are disturbingly frank. You might even regard some of these images as negative. We mentioned negative images earlier in this chapter. In reality there are no true negative images per se. This is because images reveal how you *really* feel about something at the deepest level. No matter how unappealing an image may seem, as a message from your higher self it holds out the possibility of valuable insights, opportunities for growth, and positive change.

In our view, the decoding step of the intuitive imagery process is the most fun. Images are like visual puzzles to which we apply imagination to discover the meaning. The process can be frustrating: The image may seem incomprehensible. When this occurs, remember what Erich Fromm once said: "The ability to be puzzled is the beginning of wisdom." It may also help, at these times of total dismay, to know that even great experts at image interpretation, like Carl Jung, regularly find themselves wondering at the meaning of a particular image. Jung, in fact, often would hear a dream recounted to him and have the initial reaction of total ignorance.[5] Take heart! In our experience, we have found that often the more difficult an image is to decipher, the greater is the insight it contains.

Here's another piece of advice for the interpretation step: Don't force the process. Your conscious mind may not get it, but your inner self understands the image at some deep, nonverbal level (because it sent it to your consciousness). Let go of trying to understand, and let the image simmer on the back burner of your mind. It often happens that when you let go to turn to other things, you later receive a flash of insight that reveals the meaning of the image.

When you are new to imagery work you may be tempted to refer to books that give meanings for common images and symbols. We provide a list of these resources in Appendix 3. We recognize, however, that no matter how much you may read and study and know what the "authorities" say images mean, the important meaning is what *you* make of it. Your own personal associations and meanings are what matter most. The best interpretation of any image is *always* the one that rings true to you. Have fun consulting the books, your friends, or advisers, but give the most weight to your own interpretations.

Finally, we suggest that you think of interpreting images as learning a new language, for this is what it is: you are learning the language of your inner self, or soul. Keep in mind the two Ps: patience and practice. Be patient with yourself in the beginning, and practice. Like learning Spanish, French, or COBOL, the more you practice, the more fluent you will become in making sense of what your images are saying. Practice, practice, practice until it *becomes* your practice.

STEP 5: RECORD—KEEP AN IMAGING JOURNAL

Recording is an important step in the intuitive imagery process for several reasons. First, the habit of recording the images you receive helps you identify your unique imagery language over time. This is particularly so if in your journal you add associations and feelings you have about the images you receive.

The second reason is to provide verification. We mentioned verification in chapter 3 as the final step in the four-stage creativity process. Like other types of creativity, intuitive imagery requires preparation (defining the question and relaxing), incubation (posing the question by means of a blind process and allowing images to come to mind), and illumination (insights you receive in both the image-collecting and image-interpreting stages). The last element in both creativity and intuitive imagery is to test the insight: Was it valid? Did it produce useful, trustworthy information? To see this, we suggest that you date your entries. This allows you to look back and see your progress over time. It also helps validate the results and give you confidence in the process. When clear, repeated instances of imagery prove out, you will begin to feel, as Jerry did (see chapter 5), that you can trust intuitive imagery with your life, job, fate, and future.

STEP 6: RESPOND

In the final step in the process the "rubber hits the road." You have posed your question, received images, and interpreted them. Now you must act on the information you have received. It is only by taking this step, taking action, that you test and come to trust the process. In the story of Jerry and Jean (see chapter 5), it was only because Jerry had had seven years of using intuitive imagery regularly in daily life that he *knew* he could trust it.

We suggest you build a track record yourself by use of the following steps:

1. Use intuitive imagery, acquire the guidance it offers, and record the findings in a journal (Steps 1–5).
2. Act on the guidance in concrete ways, in physical reality.
3. Record this action in your journal, with dates.
4. Return to your journal afterward, adding the results. What happened when you applied the imagery guidance?
5. Compare the outcome in reality with your imagery results: Was the imagery accurate?

Over time, as you come to see how intuitive imagery provides accurate information, you will feel able to rely on it.

NOTES

1. A set of audio tapes is available containing all these exercises; see Appendix 8.
2. This is a technique used in neurolinguistic programming (NLP).
3. Fanning 1988, 9.
4. We have drawn on several sources, including Silva 1983; Roman and Packer 1988; Buckley Seminar 1989; Saunders, 1993.
5. Cf. Jung 1965, 173; Jung 1971, 327.

7

Intuitive Imaging Guidelines

> Mental phenomena need not necessarily depend on physical laws, but rather follow laws of their own.
>
> *biologist Rupert Sheldrake*

Intuitive imaging can be done either alone or with a partner. In both cases the process uses guided imagery to engage the imagination and evoke spontaneous images and sensory input. The process is very simple. It consists of asking the person doing the imaging (the imager) a guide question—such as, "Go to a place in nature and describe what you see"—while holding the "real" question in mind without revealing it until the imaging is complete. This draws forth a purely intuitive response in the form of images, feelings, or messages that bypass the rational mind and provide profound insights that are sometimes startling in their brilliance.

More specifically, guide questions, or prompts, are used as a point of departure for the mind as it begins to receive images. The guide questions are linked mentally and energetically to a set of instructions or symbols called the *intuitive key* that is written down and/or held in the mind—but is not verbalized or shown to the imager until the imaging is done. The intuitive key represents the "real" question or intention behind the guide prompt and is the unseen focus for the intuitive mind in the imaging process. It is like a seed crystal of mental energy planted beneath the surface of the conscious mind around which spontaneous images begin to congeal and grow in the intuitive mind of the imager. Once the imaging is complete, the intuitive key is revealed and then becomes the actual "key" to unlock the meaning of the images received.

What differentiates this process from other forms of guided imagery is the blind quality of the intuitive key—it is not consciously revealed, only *mentally communicated*. This "blind" element is an essential component of intuitive imagery. We have found that it allows an individual in normal relaxed awareness to access deeper levels of mind (subconscious, unconscious, and supraconscious) through his or her intuition or direct knowing. The blind element must be maintained to temporarily disengage the logical mind, bypass normal habits of perception that limit and channel our thinking, and get beneath the ego mind—the personality issues that generate erroneous or misleading self-talk around the real question being considered (i.e., the unspoken instructions of the intuitive key).

Maintaining the blind quality is no problem when you work with a partner: You simply keep the true question to yourself. When working alone, you need to add a technique to camouflage your questions so that your logical mind will not be able to know what is really the object of the inquiry. This technique is described in this chapter along with pointers on working with a partner and choosing guide questions.

If the process sounds confusing at this point, it's only because it is still new. The examples further on in this chapter will clarify what we've described in words. And as you begin to use it, you will find that intuitive imagery is really very simple.

CHOOSING GUIDE QUESTIONS OR PROMPTS

All guided imagery processes have made use of guide questions to provide a theme or point of departure for the mind to begin to receive images. Past workers in psychotherapy, psychosynthesis, and image therapy all used a wide range of guide questions in an increasingly artful way to access the psyche and produce deep insight and personal transformation. We draw on this work in presenting the information on guide questions in this chapter, as well as on the work of Magaly Rodriguez. There is, however, a difference in both intent and application between intuitive imagery and the work of early explorers in the field of guided imagery. The objective of psychosynthesis or image therapy is healing and personal transformation. While that is certainly a powerful use of the intuitive imagery process (see chapter 9), our primary focus is on its ability to obtain practical insight and answers to the issues we face in business and everyday life. Rather than therapeutic (curative or life giving), our focus is *psychagogic*, from the Greek, meaning "guidance of the soul." In other words, we are interested in harnessing intuitive knowing in a disciplined way to produce practical results. This starts with a basic understanding of guide questions.

The purpose of a guide question is to give the mind a place to start in receiving images. The guide question is a mental hook that helps to retrieve images from the "imaginal" space beyond cognition and download them into conscious awareness for further processing. What is important is that it not be so directive that it closes down the full range of imaging possibilities. Neither is it optimum for the guide question to be so open that it doesn't provide a place to start. For instance, we could simply ask the imager, "Relax and get an image. What do you see?" This may work with experienced practitioners but is frequently less than ideal. It provides no theme or point of departure for the mind to begin and can waste time and reduce confidence as a result.

We have found it helpful when doing intuitive imagery to use guide instructions in the form of an initial directive statement that is general in nature, followed by more specific questions. For example, "See a door. What does it look like? Open it. What do you find?" or "Meet a person. Describe this person. How is he or she dressed? What do you know about this person? How do you feel about the person?"

These instructions, or prompts, give your mind a focus or framework for the session and help to relax your mind. They also help to "prime the pump" for most people. Although they are not absolutely necessary, the prompts seem to be useful in sparking images.

Your intuitive mind has available to it an almost infinite number of images from which to choose. Starting the flow of images from this infinite stream can, for some people, be like drinking from a firehose. The guide question helps to select a category, like choosing a genre for a story—adventure, mystery, romance, and so on. Once you've chosen to write an adventure story, you still need a focus for the story. That's what the intuitive key provides. The mentally or energetically communicated "intuitive key" (your real question) provides a specific intent that sorts through and chooses images that communicate a specific message (your answer) within the context of the overall adventure framework.

This can be further clarified using the following analogy. The images available to our intuitive minds are like the many different kinds of invisible electromagnetic transmissions that we can receive in our everyday environment—radio, TV, cellular phone, fax, radar, etc. Choosing a guide question is like choosing a specific channel to watch on your television. You've tuned into a particular frequency, but you still need the intuitive key to focus in on the precise program and message that is desired. That's the way the guide prompt and the intuitive key work together to bring you the information you desire. And remember, even if you don't understand how television signals are transmitted and received, you know you can turn on your TV and tune into the program you want. It's the same with intuitive imagery, especially in the beginning. You may not understand *how* it works, only that you can turn it on and it *does* work.

Turning on your images starts with choosing a guide prompt that fits your real question (intuitive key). At this point, the important thing to understand and experience about guide questions is this: They tune your mental screen to a specific channel and help get the imaging process started. If you are new to learning intuitive imagery, we urge you to sample a variety of guide questions and see how they work for you.

Here are some examples of guide questions or prompts we have used successfully in a wide array of inquiries:

- Open a door.
- Open a box.
- See a building or structure.
- See something from nature.
- Imagine a business (or organization, an activity in business, etc.).
- Imagine a room.
- Meet a person/entity.
- Meet a member of the animal kingdom (or plant kingdom, etc.).
- Go to a movie.
- Go to a place (a place in nature, a mountain top, a business, your favorite place, etc.).
- Go to the future (and/or past).
- Take a journey (take a voyage, go on a quest, etc.).
- Imagine yourself on a path.
- Walk through a gateway or portal.
- Gaze into the flames of a fire (or into a pool).
- Imagine a musical instrument.
- See a vehicle.
- Become _____ (a character, a business, an animal, a river, a fire, the wind, the earth, etc.). What do you know?
- Discover something (receive/give a gift, etc.).
- Get a message (spoken, written, or otherwise communicated).
- Open a book and read something.
- Tell a brief story.
- Hear some music (a song, a speech, a chant).
- Feel something. What emotions/sensations are present?

These are just a sampling. You can create your own or vary these in any number of ways; the only limit is your imagination.

Remember, the purpose of the guide questions is to assist your mind in producing images that hold clues to answering your question. For optimum results, however, it helps to fit the type of prompt with the primary imaging modality of the imager—yourself or your partner.

Most people are visual and have no trouble receiving images. So visual prompts work well in most cases ("go to a place," "open a door," etc.). But some are primarily auditory or primarily kinesthetic. Auditory types work better with receiving messages, or hearing the information. Kinesthetic types work best with sensations and emotions. Sometimes, you need to give yourself or partner permission to use their imagination to "just make up a response." When coauthor John does imaging, he frequently just "knows" the answer before he ever sees an image.

In our experience, some prompts are more useful for answering certain questions than others. The following are specific situations in which a particular prompt is apt:

Open a Door This is a good general imaging guide that works well for most issues. By asking what the door looks like, what is behind it, what story it contains, what you know about the images you received, you produce multiple clues that offer insights to your question. If you are confronting a question involving choices in your life or business, you can vary this prompt by changing the guide question to "see a series of doors." Assign each door to an individual choice; number them; then notice to which one you are most drawn.

See a Box This is a variation on the door prompt. Additional questions provide more information: How big is the box? Is it wrapped or plain? What is in it? When you are facing several options, ask, for example, "To which box am I most drawn?" or "Which box is biggest?" Seeing a series of boxes and choosing the one to which you are most drawn is a good way to choose among a series of options.

See a Structure (or Series of Structures)　In this prompt, *structure* can be anything that is constructed and has a specific form, tangible or intangible, such as a building, cup, suitcase, starship, computer, robot, communication network (information structure), organizational structure, and so on. With this prompt you can receive more information by asking how large the structure is (or which is largest if you are seeing a series), what the surroundings look like, what the foundation is like, or what goes on here. Sometimes interesting insights emerge if you *become* the structure. Then ask "What do you know? What is your perspective?" The resulting answers are often very different from how your left-brain consciousness sees the situation. This guide question is very useful for looking at a person, an organization, or the structure of a relationship.

Meet a Person　The person you meet in your imagination can be anyone—a wise person, a friend, a character out of legend or fantasy, a mystical or religious figure, or a Klingon warrior. Don't censor what comes into your imagination; allow whatever image comes into your mind's eye. Then describe the person—how he or she looks, what the clothes are like, and so on. Note what you know about the person and how you feel about him or her. Ask yourself what strengths and weaknesses stand out and what you know about the person's purpose or mission in life. This guide question is useful when you want a look at yourself, other people, organizations, or competitors. There's a caution with this prompt: As discussed in chapter 6, imagery can be frank, so be prepared to see things about yourself that you may not have anticipated.

Get a Message　This type of guide question works well for people who are auditory. A nice way to use this prompt is to imagine meeting a wise person who gives you a message. The image you receive and its message are often from your Higher Self or a Higher Source. This prompt is a good way to gain insight on what the next steps are in a process that is under way.

Go to a Place and Look Around   Describe the locale, sur-roundings, any object, people, or structures of which you are aware. This is a good prompt for examining a business or organi-zation or for gaining a sense of where you are in your life. Vari-ations can be quite numerous, as can be seen in the previous listing of guide questions. Just *where* you ask someone to go in his or her imagination can deepen the imaging response. For in-stance, asking someone to "go down underground" or "go into a closet" or "explore the darkness" may help turn up hidden or buried issues. Alternately, asking someone to "go to a mountain top" or to "walk into the light" may assist in getting to a higher perspective or more enlightened view of the issue in question. Guide questions work best when they are metaphors for the kind of information you are looking for.

Imagine Yourself on a Path   This prompt is useful espe-cially when you have an objective or goal to reach. Ask yourself what the path looks like: Is it bumpy or smooth, level or uphill? How hard is it to travel? Are there any blocks or obstacles? Any aids? Where does it take you? You can amplify this question, to gain additional insight, by prompting yourself to find several things along the way. What do you find? This imagery exercise will produce information about what the path to achieving your goal looks like. It is also good for evaluating choices or strategies.

Discover Something   What you discover in this exercise is anything that stands out or draws your attention. This discovery does not have to be something material; it can be intangible, like love, happiness, or a black cloud. You can glean more data by prompting yourself to find several things of value. Describe each one. What do you know about it? What is it used for? Why is it valuable? Answering these questions often provides insights about what is unique in a situation or what is needed to trans-form a situation.

Table 7.1 lists possible situations and the type of prompt questions you might pose.

Table 7.1   Life Situations and Possible Prompt Questions

Situation or need	Prompt question
General	Open a door or box What do you find? Describe what you see
To choose among options	See a series of doors or boxes To which one are you most drawn? Which box is largest?
To examine a person, organization or business, or the structure of a relationship	See a structure What is it? What goes on here? What is its perspective?
To look at yourself, other people, an organization or business, or competitor	Meet a person How does the person look? How do you feel about the person? What strengths or weaknesses are obvious?
To gain insight into the next steps in a process (good for persons primarily auditory rather than visual)	Get a message
To gain a sense of where you or a business or organization is in life	Go to a place and look around Where are you? What do you see?
To evaluate choices or strategies or to see what the path to achieving a goal looks like	Imagine yourself on a path What does it look like? Is it hard or easy to travel? Are there any obstacles or aids? Where does it take you?
To see what is unique in a situation or to identify what is needed to transform a situation	Find something, or several things, of value What did you find? What do you know about it? What is it used for? Why is it valuable?

(Continued)

Table 7.1 Life Situations and Possible Prompt Questions *(continued)*

Situation or need	*Prompt question*

To gauge how accurately you are seeing the future	Go to a place and look in front of you
	    What do you see, hear, feel or
	      know?
	    How clear are your images?

To determine your mission in life	See yourself on a road
	    What does this road look like?
	    What does this road contain as
	      features?
	    How clearly do you see it?
	    What is your destination?

The following are examples of how to use guide questions. The variations are limited only by your own creativity.

Intuitive Key: A Place That Represents Your Life

Today. *(This guide question can also be used to receive images that provide insight about your business, workplace, organization, or relationships, to name a few of the possibilities. Change the intuitive key to fit your question and the images will change to provide you with the answer.)*

1a. **Guide:** Go to a place and look around. Describe what you see.

Intuitive Key: An Image of the Past. *(Frequently, it is helpful to take a look at the past to explore the roots of the current situation.)*

1b. **Guide:** Let the image shift as you travel backwards in time. Now what do you see, feel, hear, know?

Intuitive Key: An Image of the Future. *(Imaginal space is very flexible. You will find that the imager is able to move through time. Exploring the future is a good way to see potential outcomes to the current situation. The clarity and vivid-*

ness of the imagery you receive also will tell you how clearly you are seeing the future.)

1c. **Guide:** Let the image in your mind shift again as you travel forward in time to the future. Now what do you see, feel, hear, know?

Intuitive Key: A Person That Represents Your Business, a Quest That Symbolizes its Purpose.

(The clarity of the images may show how well you understand your business or its purpose. How attainable the quest is or how close the person is to achieving it will also give additional insight. This guide prompt can also be used to get insight on clients, competition, or, on a personal level, your own mission.)

2a. **Guide:** Meet a person on a quest. Describe the person and his or her quest.

Intuitive Key: A Gift the Business Brings to the World.
(What the person gives you can be used to symbolize whatever you designate them to be in your intuitive key, as long as it fits as an extension to the key in 2a. Other possibilities include what your client has to give you; competitor xyz's strength in the market; or the gift that you personally bring to the world.)

2b. **Guide:** This person gives you something. What is it?

Intuitive Key: The Path That the Business Is on.
(How easy the path is to travel will give insight into the business and whether it is in for a difficult time. Barriers on the path represent barriers to the business. Again, this guide question could be used with a different intuitive key to look at clients, competitors, or personal path.)

2c. **Guide:** See the path this person is on. Describe how easy it is to travel. What barriers do you find?

Intuitive Key: A Structure That Represents Yourself.
(You can also designate the structure to represent someone you want to gain insight about. Asking additional guide ques-

tions will then provide additional insight. For instance, as a follow-up you can ask: What do you like about the structure? What could be improved? What does the foundation look like? As with other examples, different intuitive keys can be used to look at the structure of a business or relationship, an actual physical structure, or even the health of the physical body.)

3a. **Guide:** See structure. Describe what you see.

Intuitive Key: More Information. *(This is a powerful technique borrowed from Gestalt psychology. The structure exists as "real" in imaginal space. As the persons doing the imaging "become" the structure in their minds, they also become more closely linked with whatever the structure designates in the intuitive key of 3a, and a whole new level of insight is available to them. Another technique is to ask the imager to "dialogue" with the image to gain additional information—for example, ask the image what it knows.)*

3b. **Guide:** Become the structure. What do you know?

Intuitive Key: An Image of Yourself in the Future. *(This is an important and flexible technique. It can be used to dig down into an issue. Building on an initial question, you can change intuitive keys and merely ask the imager to "blink," then ask, "What happens to the image now?" You will find that the images received will shift as your hidden question shifts. This is the kind of thing that can fill you with awe as you experience it for the first time.)*

3c. **Guide:** Mentally blink your eyes, allowing the image to shift. What happens?

DOING INTUITIVE IMAGERY ALONE

As discussed in chapters 3 and 4, the left brain is dominant in our culture. When we want to get at the wisdom contained in the right brain, we have to use special processes—meditation, reverie, creativity techniques, or intuitive imagery with an intuitive key. This bypasses the rational mind temporarily and makes the process "blind." Your left brain does not know the question for which you are receiving images, and the result is images uncontaminated by ego, anxiety, attachments, old ideas or habits of thinking, or fear. If you are working alone, however, how can your left brain not know the question you are posing to your right brain? By the use of *multiple questions.*

The following are the steps in doing intuitive imagery solo:

1. Define your question. This is just as we described in chapter 6, but here you think of several questions (at least 3 or 4), and write each question on the back of an index card, *one question per card.* This step creates the intuitive key to interpreting your images. By having several images, your left brain will not be able to identify which question you are dealing with as you work through the process.

2. Choose an imaging guide prompt in advance. Before you begin receiving images, choose a prompt that will work for the questions you developed in Step 1. This guide question should have something to do with your inquiry. See Table 7.1 for tips to which guide prompts are most suited to elicit which type of information. If you have several different types of questions, group them into batches that will work with the same prompt.

In this step you can create additional questions by creating additional references. For example, suppose you want to identify what is needed to transform the troublesome relationship your business is having with client X. To make the process blind, you can pose this same question for three additional clients, A, B, and C. These four would then become four questions with the same prompt. Write each question on a separate card, and then do the imagery. A note of caution: You are likely to gain insights that may surprise you not only about client X but also about the other clients. Be sure you are ready and willing to receive this information.

3. Turn the cards face down and write the guide question on each card. (Note: The process works best with colored index cards. With white ones, it is too tempting to read your question through the back. This destroys the intuitive power of the process.)

4. Shuffle the cards until you have no idea which question is on which index card; then number each card. Keep them all face down until the imagery process for all the cards is completed.

5. Relax and receive images. Pick up the first card on the pile and, *without turning it over,* hold it in your hand. Relax and center yourself, if necessary, using one or more of the relaxation exercises mentioned in chapter 6. Allow yourself to receive images and sensory reactions. Record your images and feelings, either on the card itself or on a separate pad on which you have written the number of the card. Do this for each card.

There are a variety of optional methods for receiving images. You don't have to record your images in writing; if it seems more appropriate or comfortable, you can draw or sketch a picture, or create a story or myth about the images. You may also image animals that provide insight into your answer, or that amplify the images you received in response to the prompt question.

6. Interpret your images. The next step is to interpret your images in reference to the original question (see chapter 8). To do this, turn over the cards and match the intuitive key question with the images. Next, work on decoding. You may want to consult reference books and imagery experts, but as mentioned in chapter 6, *you* are the best interpreter of your own images, and *your* associations and meanings are most important.

7. Date and record your results in a journal. The final step in intuitive imagery is verification. We suggest the following format for doing this:

Date: (the day on which you did the imagery)
Intuitive Key: (your question, underlined)
The Guide Prompt: (for example, "See a structure")
Your Images: (what you received, in visual, sensory, or auditory information)

Your Interpretation: (how you related the images to the original question)

Results: (leave space to record, at a later date, what actions you took in response to the imagery guidance and what then happened for comparison with the imaging information)

Here are some examples, from our own lives, of solo intuitive imagery in practice:

Date: September 29, 1992

Intuitive Key 1: A Place That Represents Your Business Organization

Guide 1: Go to a place from your life. Describe it and how you feel there.

Image 1: I [John] am in a boat, a cabin cruiser. It is headed out to sea in the wake of a turbulent outgoing tide. I am turning the wheel furiously, attempting to turn the boat around and head back to shore. The rudder is not responding. The boat is still being carried out to sea. I have to choose whether to be carried out with it or jump into the surf and swim for shore. The shore is not that far away but I'm not sure I can swim well enough to make it. I am afraid but I have to decide quickly.

Interpretation: There is a great deal of turbulence in the business. I have to decide whether to be carried along with it or to jump ship and swim toward freedom. I'm not sure I can make it on my own.

Intuitive Key 2: A Person or Entity That Is a Symbol of Your Higher Purpose in Life

Guide 2: Meet a person or entity in this place. Describe him or her and what you know about him or her.

Image 2: A dolphin jumping out of the water. She is swimming near the boat. I know she will help me get to the shore.

Interpretation: Dolphins are a traditional saver of the ship-wrecked and a guide. They represent safety in troubled waters. I am being told that my Higher Path lies in jumping ship. I will be guided to safety.

Results: At the time I received these images, there was a great deal of turmoil in DuPont because of a large downsizing effort (the outgoing tide). These images resulted in my asking for and receiving a separation package from DuPont. I left at the end of 1992 to start my own business. Since leaving, I have felt gently guided to take each new step.

DOING INTUITIVE IMAGERY WITH A PARTNER

The intuitive imagery process is the same when working with a partner or several people, but it has several advantages. It is interactive, which can provide more information and insight into your question, and you can ask the specific question you are after, without the need to pose several to keep the process blind. Just be sure you keep the subject of your inquiry to yourself, so your friend (or friends) has no conscious clue what you are asking about.

The following are the steps when doing intuitive imagery with another person:

1. Ask permission. Never do intuitive imagery without informing your partner what you are up to. Obtain prior agreement from them to use their images for shedding light on your question.

2. Review the ground rules. If your partners are new to imagery, help them to understand that their imagination is not bound by the ordinary physical laws of nature. Simply stated, this means that they can levitate, fly, teleport, go under water without breathing, read minds, walk through fire, or anything else that they can conjure up in their minds. Give them permission to imagine freely. Some people need it. And tell them not to be surprised or frightened if unusual things occur. Alternatively, if no images come to their minds, give them permission to just make something up—whatever first comes to mind.

3. Define the question. Refer to chapter 6 for tips on how to formulate a clear question. Remember that this step is a key to receiving a useful answer. A quality question is essential to producing a quality answer.

4. Select a suitable guide question. You can use those suggested in Table 7.1, or you can create your own. It can be anything you like—doors, places, paths, books, boxes, and so on.

5. Guide your partner. Give the initial guide instruction, such as "Please go to a place and look around. Describe what you see." (In this example, the place the partner sees represents your question.) Then record the images as your partner speaks. If you have more than one person receiving images, it works best if each writes down his or her image, rather than speaking out loud.

6. Interpret the images. This step differs a bit from the interpretation phase of solo work, because it is interactive. When you work with someone else's images, his or her interpretation of the images is often more important than your own. So you must work together to decode the imagery and relate it to your original question.

7. Record the imagery. As with solo work, record what you received in a dated journal entry, leaving space to record later what action you took and what resulted from applying the imagery guidance.

EXERCISE: A SAMPLE OF SOLO INTUITIVE IMAGERY

Like most practical skills in life, intuitive imagery has to be learned by doing it. In this section we want to guide you through the first four steps of the solo process (the fifth step, interpreting, is discussed in chapter 8). Get some paper and a pencil or pen and try intuitive imagery for yourself.

Step 1: Choose a Guide Question   Refer to Table 7.1, in which are listed a variety of situations in life and their related prompt questions. One of these nine areas is likely to relate to the questions or concerns you have. You can use an almost unlimited number of variations if the guide questions we offer don't appeal to you. The key is to choose one that works well for the type of concern into which you want insight. If, for example, you want to examine your business corporation, you would choose the guide question "See a structure."

Step 2: Write the Questions into Which You Want Insight   In solo work, these need to be multiple questions, at least three or more. In the example:

> **Question 1:** A structure that represents *my business corporation*
>
> **Question 2:** A structure that represents *my relationship with my spouse*
>
> **Question 3:** A structure that represents *my physical body and its current state of health*

Try this in the space below, with a prompt and three questions of your own:

> Guide Question 1: _____
>
> Question/Issue 1: _____
>
> Question/Issue 2: _____
>
> Question/Issue 3: _____

Step 3: Do the Solo Intuitive Imagery Process   Copy your three questions onto three separate index cards. Turn the cards face down. Write the guide question on the facing side. Shuffle the cards until you don't know which question is on which card. Number each card. Receive images for each card in turn (no peeking!).

Repeat this process for a second guide question:

Guide Question 2: _____

Question/Issue 1: _____

Question/Issue 2: _____

Question/Issue 3: _____

The next step is to interpret the images you received. This is the subject of chapter 8.

8

Guidelines for Interpreting Images

> The most beautiful thing we can experience is the mysterious. It is the source of all true art and science.
>
> *Albert Einstein*

This step, the decoding of images, provides the most fun. It is challenging, puzzling, and makes possible great insights into yourself, other people, your life and business. As we noted in earlier chapters, interpreting images successfully requires two things: being open to receiving unexpected, perhaps unpalatable information and letting go in the face of an incomprehensible image, rather than trying to force the process.

Interpreting images is like learning a language. Fluency in translating the imagery language of the right brain comes only with practice. It can, however, be made easier if you follow certain guidelines and use the time-tested techniques discussed in this chapter.

GENERAL TIPS

The first tip is something we must repeat from chapters 6 and 7. *You* are the best authority on the meaning of your own images. If you are new to imagery work you may not believe this, but it is true. Your right brain sends up the images you receive from your unconscious, and your Higher Self knows they are meaningful. We have seen, in our own experience and from working with hundreds of people in imagery workshops, that you *can* discover your own expertise and feel comfortable trusting your interpretations.

The second general tip is a reminder that at the interpretation phase, imagery work is all of a piece. If you already do imagery interpretation in other contexts—the decoding of images, pictures, scenes, or stories in art, literary criticism, or iconography—you will find the interpretation step a familiar process. If you do dreamwork or regularly analyze your dreams, you will be able to apply the same interpretative techniques here.

The more you know about yourself, the easier it is to evaluate your images. This is because when you know yourself well, you are more conscious of the unconscious, the source of imagery. So its products are more familiar.

Your goal in the interpretation phase is to achieve understanding and knowledge—of yourself, your business, or your issue—not accuracy. This process is not a test, and objectivity is not necessary. Your personal, subjective meanings, associations, and insights are more important than being "right." Don't be afraid to be wrong, for, in reality, there *is* no wrong. We have found imagery interpretation to be self-correcting. If you misinterpret one image, another one will often get the message through. The key here is not correctness or accuracy, but making the effort. Attending to the process—making the effort—activates your Higher Self, giving you hidden levels of support.

Keep a record of your imagery interpretations. We emphasize in chapters 6 and 7 the value of keeping a journal. Here is another reason to do so. By keeping a record, you will gain lasting information about your own personal imagery language. Over time, you will see patterns emerge that will make decoding easier. For example, after one man worked for some time with his images, he found that he often received an image of a lively, playful dog. He came to discover that it referred to his emerging new life with its youthful energies. Only by recording such images in a journal will you be able to return to them later and over time build up your unique image-language dictionary.

Another general tip bears repeating from earlier chapters: be open. This is easy to say, but we have found it difficult for many people to do, and closed-mindedness is a big reason why people don't "get" what their imagery is saying. They don't really want to hear its message. Because images come from deeper levels of mind beyond ego consciousness, they often present information that threatens our conscious self-image, belief system, or assumptions about reality. It is natural that we try to hold on to these beliefs (since they served us well at some point), but images call us to new life. They demand that we grow, and personal growth requires being open to the promptings of our inner wisdom.

A final general tip is to apply what imagery offers as guidance. When you interpret images, you are melding right-brain intuition with left-brain reason and analysis. After you examine rationally the information you have received from imagery, ask yourself if some concrete action is appropriate. For example, in light of the guidance of your imagery, do you need to change something in your life? Get out of the company you are in? Leave a bad relationship? Ask your broker for more information? Change your business strategy? Applying what you glean from imagery sessions is important because doing so tells the mind that you are serious. It keeps the channels open for you to receive more intuitive wisdom. It provides deeper levels of meaning, validation, and confidence, and it brings you, eventually, a richer, more meaningful, more fulfilling life.

TOOLS AND TECHNIQUES FOR INTERPRETING IMAGERY[1]

Pose Some Questions

A variety of types of questions can help to ferret out the meaning of an image. We offer a review of several types.

Basic Starter Questions   You can begin by posing questions about the image itself. How bright is it? How much light is there? How close or far away is it? Does anything about it stand out? Is there anything unusual about it? What does the image do? How does it work? What is it used for? Ask yourself if you have had this image before in imagery work, a dream, or a meditation. Finally, consider if there is there a relation between this image and other images you have had.

Bring in Your Senses   You can ask questions about the image and the imagery experience that draw on your senses. How do I feel about this image? What emotions come up for me? What sounds do I hear? What colors do I see?

Relate the Image to Yourself   Consider your personal reactions to the image. Ask questions such as, How do I react to the image physically? What body sensations do I associate with it? Where in my body do I feel this image? Does this image trigger a memory of someone or something? With what do I associate this image? What do the colors mean to me (if the image had colors)? What part am I playing in the image? If all parts of the image represented me, what would these parts be saying about me? Is there anything in my life now that the image reminds me of? Is the image an important symbol for me? (We discuss archetypal symbols in chapter 9.) You can also pose evaluative questions.

Questions to Evaluate the Image   These questions bring your own subjective tastes and preferences to bear on the imagery. For example, If there are colors in the images, are they pleasing or displeasing? What is appealing about the image? What is unappealing? Are there any puns in the image? Puns can be visual (like a cartoon) or verbal (coming out of your verbal description of the image or what is going on in it). The Higher Self, in our experience, delights in humor, and we have found a close connection between the *ha-ha* of humor and the *aha* of discovery. An example of an imagery pun:

A woman was at the point of changing careers, wondering if she was meant to stay in teaching, and received an image of teaching a school of *fish*. That image told her a great deal—she didn't think very highly of her students—and she left teaching soon thereafter.

A final element to evaluate is the idiomatic phrases in your description of the image. An example illustrates how this works:

I [Sue] did imagery seeking insight into a relationship. I was given the image of being on a roller coaster, and as the imagery developed I saw that I was being *taken for a ride*. It had a literal truth, in that I was not running the roller coaster myself, but this particular phrase also has a wider meaning in English, a meaning that gave me great insight into my true feelings about the relationship.

We suggest that you watch for such verbal or visual puns and phrases, and evaluate them in light of your original inquiry. They often can give you profound insights.

Dialogue with the Image   A final type of questioning is posed to the image itself, as if it were a person. This is a technique borrowed from Gestalt therapy that can provide additional information. Ask the image for its meaning. Ask it what it wants from you, what action it might want you to consider. Try becoming the image and then ask: What do I, as the image, know? How do I feel? What message do I have?

Deciphering Techniques

Working with Multiple Images   If you have to decipher multiple images, you have a choice. You can work with each one separately, or you can treat them all together and extract the basic theme they share. If you choose the latter option, try to limit a statement of the theme to one sentence. This technique often gives you a broad overview of the meaning of the image.

Consult Reference Works or Authorities   If your image is or contains symbols, they may be in the sources we list in Appendix 3. If you use such references, we urge you to take only the meaning or interpretation that rings true for you. This advice is equally valid when working with authorities, like Jungian analysts or transpersonal and archetypal therapists, because *your own judgment* is best. The task of interpretation is not something that can be handed over to others to do for you.

The Ratings Scale   This technique is useful when you are dealing with images related to choices or options. Use a ratings scale of 1 to 10 (10 = best) to get a feel for the relative value of various options or to assign priorities. Another variant of this technique is to visualize a bar chart and let the relative sizes of the bars stand for the importance of the options. This method is particularly useful when you face choosing among two, three, or four options.

Word Association   This technique is a way to unpack the meaning of intuitive contents by use of the left brain. Originally developed by Sigmund Freud to get at the meaning of dreams, word association is applicable to decoding the meaning of any symbol. As befits a left-brain activity, it is a linear process in which the meaning of one word or image triggers another thought, which then triggers another, until "Aha!" is reached, and the real meaning becomes clear. This process works because left-brain thinking is associative and naturally creates chains of association. The following is an example of word association:

work → play → actor → star → sun → light → bulb → tulips → kiss → love → tennis → net → profit → prophet → oracle → auricle → heart → life[2]

Here is how word association can look when used to decipher the meaning of images:

In October of 1994, I [John] asked in a solo imaging session what my life partner needed most from me. I received two images. The first was a large pipe organ in a cathedral. The second was a flag. My word associations for each of these was as follows:

pipe organ → choir → singing → music → sound → voice
flag → country → boundaries → sovereignty → personal power

As it turned out, these two images were not unrelated. What my partner needed from me was to help provide the encouragement and space for her to get back into singing and move deeper into the study of the therapeutic uses of sound. This was part of her discovering her personal power and attaining a new sense of sovereignty. She had recently been reunited with her college voice teacher who was retiring after 30 years. He was asking my partner to sing the soprano solo to Verdi's *Requiem* in a special recording session (mid 1995). Rehearsing for this moved her back into singing and the study of sound and brought her back in touch with her unique vocal talent that had lain dormant for many years. This set in motion a series of synchronistic events that resulted in her beginning the deeper study of sound and vibration with a Native American shaman in early 1996.

This example shows how word associations can work. Images are very concentrated, powerful forms of communication that contain many bits of information, but they have to be decoded or unpacked. Letting your mind associate around the image is one way to unpack them to reveal their hidden meanings. See Appendix 6 for practice exercises with word association.

Word Amplification   Similar to word association in its origins in psychology, word amplification was developed by Carl Jung, the Swiss psychiatrist and founder of analytical psychology. This technique is less linear than word association. Whereas in word association, one idea leads to another, in word amplification, you build on the central symbol, adding connecting thoughts as they come to you. Each thought goes back to the original image, and each time you make an association, you go back to the original symbol to get the next thought. The result is more a cluster of thoughts than a line. The key to word amplification is to suspend judgment and allow ideas to flow freely. Become childlike in giving your imagination free play, and see how many ideas you can connect with the central symbol before the true meaning pops out for you. The following is an example of how we have used word amplification, in this case to predict the future state of the economy:

> In February of 1989 I asked, "What will the state of the U.S. economy be in 1990?" The image I received was of a river running into a cave, which was at the foot of a gigantic tree. This imagery exercise gave me three images to interpret: the river, the cave, and the tree. Using word amplification to decode these images might look like Figure 8.1.
>
> On the basis of my amplifications, I came up with the following interpretation. In the image, the river represented the U.S. economy. It was flowing *into* the cave, which was at the foot of the tree. The interpretation seems clear. The flow of the economy was headed for a descent. Its life force would return to the womb leading to a rebirth at a later date. The gigantic tree is another image of the U.S. economy showing its size—the largest in the world. Yet the tree also stood at the mouth of the cave, indicating that the economy's strength and growth would pull within. In fact, the U.S. economy *did* enter a recession in 1990. Later imaging qualified the magnitude of the recession, predicting a three to five percent decline, which was right on target.

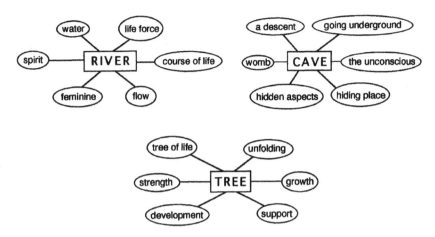

Figure 8.1 Word Amplification Diagram

See Appendix 6 for exercises with word amplification.

Incubate the Image Another technique that often helps with difficult images is incubation. Hold the index card on which you wrote the image (if you did solo imaging), and let the image incubate in your mind. Write down any insights you experience. If nothing comes, or you want further information, ask your Higher Self to send you information in your dreams or meditations about what the meaning might be.

Guess at the Meaning This technique, which we put far down on the list of ways to tackle interpretation, is something you might be tempted to do *first*, but we suggest trying it as a next-to-last resort. After you have tried some of the other methods, you can make a guess, but it will be an *educated* rather than a blind guess. Assume you know what the meaning is (you do, after all, as it was *your* image). So ask yourself, if you did know, what would it be?

Let Go and Allow the Image to Simmer This is the last resort. Give up trying to figure it out. Turn to other things. Go play. In our experience it is likely that, at some unexpected moment, you will experience a flash of insight that gives you the meaning.

Use Imaging to Gain More Information   This is an advanced technique that you can begin to use once you've learned the basic process. It is very effective, particularly when you are working interactively with a partner. If you want additional insight into the meaning of an image, simply guide your partner to "Open a door" or "Blink your mental eyes, let the image shift, and tell me what happens." (As you work with a partner more, you can shorten this cue to just, "Blink. What happens now?") While asking the guide question, mentally hold the thought, "More information" or "Additional insight," as your intuitive key. Alternately, you can take a guess at the meaning of the original image and use that as your intuitive key (e.g., Guide: Open a door; Intuitive Key: Does this image mean ____?). Using this process, you can continue opening doors (or doing additional "blinks") until the meaning of the initial image is clear. The technique works well. It does, however, give you additional images to interpret using the guidelines we've already outlined.

DEALING WITH YES OR NO QUESTIONS

In chapter 6 we referred to the simplest type of imagery question, yes or no. Should I go to the sales meeting in Denver? Should I ask for a raise? There are two ways to handle such questions: using the usual method or taking a shortcut.

Using the Usual Imagery Method

Use the intuitive imagery process to elicit uncensored images. Then evaluate the imagery to determine whether you are receiving a *yes* or a *no*. We've found an interpretive technique used by Tony Robbins in neurolinguistic programming (NLP) to be effective in this regard.[3] The guidelines are simple:

A *Yes* Answer Is Likely When the Image looks pleasing or appealing, feels good emotionally or kinesthetically, or is uplifting, joyful, or inspirational. "Yes" answers may make you laugh, or feel lighter. In fact, the colors are usually lighter and brighter. The images themselves will, as a general rule, be easier to "see" in your imagination, resulting in a clear, well-defined mental picture. The context that the image is in may be more orderly, peaceful, or harmonious. And frequently it will appear in a more natural setting. Images of butterflies flitting from flower to flower, a child running playfully across a field of flowers, a beautiful sunrise or sunset, a pleasing romance, a wise and friendly person, or discovering a treasure chest are all examples of positive, "Yes" answers.

The Answer May Be *No* When the Image looks dark, dangerous, unattractive, and unappealing, when it is *not* pleasing. "No" answers may not feel good, may bring up an uneasy sense of anxiety, may feel heavy and depressing. Or, the image may be hard to see, indistinct, or have muddy colors. The image may appear in context that is chaotic, unfriendly, inharmonious, violent, or artificial. Images of war or fighting or struggle, a tarantula crawling out of a dark corner, a skeleton, feeling frightened in a dark cave, an explosion, or getting a depressing message are all examples of negative, "No" answers.

Take a Shortcut

This is a five-step process.

> **Step 1:** Write the question for which you want an answer on a pad of paper.
>
> **Step 2:** Write *Yes* and *No* on two separate pieces of paper.
>
> **Step 3:** Fold both papers so that the *Yes* and *No* are invisible.
>
> **Step 4:** Shuffle the papers.

Step 5: Choose between the two by means of one of the following methods:

Imagine which one steps forward.

Imagine a bar chart in your mind with bars corresponding to the two choices. Which bar is higher? That is the correct choice.

Receive a message about which piece of paper is the right choice (this is especially good for auditory types).

Hold the two pieces of paper, one in each hand. Instruct yourself that the hand holding the correct choice will become lighter and rise.

Imagine that the correct choice lights up.

Imagine a rose bud in front of each choice. The rose in front of the best choice blooms while the other wilts and droops over.

If you are kinesthetic, use your hand to scan the energy in each response. Choose the one which has the most energy.

If none of these methods appeals to you, you can design an intuitive system that works for you.

VALIDATION TECHNIQUES

The final element in interpreting images is validation: Is my interpretation correct? How can I tell? Certain ways to do so are mentioned earlier—the ring of truth, the flash of insight. When you experience these moments, you understand what St. Exupery meant when he said that truth is ineluctable.[4] It really *is* that which cannot be escaped. It grabs you or catches you and there is no doubt about it. You *know* your interpretation is correct. Not every imagery interpretation has this quality, however. With some you will need to apply other criteria. Here are some we have found useful:

The Test of Feeling   Consider how you feel about the image. Do you feel light or uplifted (true) or heavy and down (false)?

The Visualization Test   Ask yourself, "Is this information true?" Then visualize a yes or a no response.

The Test from Content   Consider the quality underlying the content of the imagery. Truth is simple, caring, whole-making, reconciling, reliable, and effective. Does your imagery have these qualities?

The Test of Common Sense   Imagery comes from your intuition. It is part of the left-brained bias of our culture that intuition is often associated with impracticality, nonsense, or foolishness. In reality, intuition is as commonsensical, grounded, and practical as anything the left brain has to offer. Use your common sense to ask, "If I accept as true what I think this image is saying and act on its guidance, what would be the consequences?" If the answer is nonsense or would entail grave negative consequences, you probably have misinterpreted the image. In all the intuitive imagery work we have done ourselves, and have heard about from hundreds of other people, the information that comes through from your Higher Self is *always* for your benefit. It may be discomfiting (especially if your life is out of line with your true purpose), but it is never destructive.

But we don't ask you to take our word on this. Test it for yourself. Practice using intuitive imagery. Work on interpreting the images you receive. Keep a journal with dated entries. Go back to your journal periodically and read over your entries. Add notes on the results you obtained and how valid your interpretations were. In this way you will build confidence in yourself and your ability to speak the language of imagery. You will come to recognize which interpretive techniques work best for you. And you will come to know you can trust the intuitive imagery process and your own inner wisdom.

You will also gain an additional benefit. You will come to know yourself as an integral part of the All, the collective wisdom of humanity. This wisdom is often conveyed imagistically in archetypes, or energy symbols. We consider some of these, and how you can work with them, in chapter 9.

NOTES

1. Many of these techniques can be found in Williams 1980; Reed 1994; Mossman 1987.
2. von Oech 1992.
3. These guidelines were also used by Mossman in "Light Imagery Work," 1987.
4. Quoted in Harman 1988, 61.

9

Working with Energy Symbols for Transformation

Contrary to what everyone knows is so, it may not be the brain that produces consciousness—but rather, consciousness that creates the appearance of the brain, matter, space, time, and everything else we are pleased to interpret as the physical universe.

psychologist Keith Floyd

In chapters 5 through 8 we introduced intuitive imagery and explained how to use it to understand the image programs we hold in our minds. These inner images shape our lives in powerful ways. They affect our feelings, our relationships, our creativity, our capabilities, the decisions we make, the level of success we achieve in business and personal life, and even our health.

The goal up to this point has been understanding and greater self-awareness. Indeed, intuitive imagery is a powerful tool to tap our reservoir of inner wisdom and produce deeper insight than the rational mind alone can give.

As we turn to working with energy symbols, our goal becomes something more creative: to *transform* and *improve* our lives and our businesses by working consciously with our inner

115

images. This is possible for two reasons. First, what we are calling *energy* symbols represent "principal ideas"—similar to Plato's conception of an ideal plane as the framework out of which the physical world unfolds. These symbols are generally ancient, and have common meanings in diverse cultures around the world. As such they become "archetypes" or models that store energy that shapes behavior and affects the physical world, much like Sheldrake's morphogenetic fields (see chapter 3). You can think of these principal ideas or energy symbols as capacitors that store energy that is available for us to use for transforming our lives. Yet, we have to be able to tap into this source of energy. How do we do this?

The second important point tells us how: We can use images to transform the issues we are dealing with because imagination and inner images link us directly to the energy source. As much as our culture has come to deify the intellect, the rational mind alone is not creative. It is analytical but not generative. It is our imagination, our intuition, our inner images that represent the closest connection with our own source, that creative, generative part of us where transformational potential exists. Our imagination is the bridge to the unconscious and superconscious where this energy exists. Our inner images provide the mental circuit which hooks into the power source of these energy symbols. Images are fundamental and powerful, and represent the natural language of the mind and body.

The word *horse* in English, *caballo* in Spanish, or *lóshaht* in Russian all represent an image of one of those four-legged beasts that we can saddle up and ride into the sunset. The image is constant. The words change. That's because words are what we make up to represent a more fundamental image. It is our inner images that are *primary*. They are the basic programming language of our human computer. As such, images come before and are more powerful than words in "speaking" to the deepest levels of our being. In fact, there is evidence to show that our *inner* images are more powerful than what we see "out there."

Robert Kunzendorf found that when he hooked subjects up to an electroencephalograph (EEG) and shined a colored light into their eyes, their brainwaves showed distinct patterns for each of the different colors.[1] A red light could be related to a red brainwave pattern, a blue light to a blue brainwave pattern, and so on. Interestingly, these brainwave patterns could be reproduced by simply asking the subject to *imagine* a color. For example, asking a subject simply to imagine the color blue produced the characteristic brainwave pattern for blue. This demonstrated that inner images produce the same response as external stimuli. But which stimulus is more primary? Kunzendorf next asked his subjects to imagine one color while he shined a different colored light into their eyes. Amazingly, it was the imagined color that showed up in the brainwave pattern recorded by the EEG. For example, if subjects were asked to imagine the color blue while a red light was flashed in their eyes, the brainwave patterns produced were for the color blue, *not* the color red. This says that *what we imagine is more real than what we see outside us.*

Although this concept may seem startling at first, it makes sense in light of recent discoveries. Neurophysiologists now know that the visual information that we receive via our optic nerves is first filtered through our temporal lobes, where it is edited and modified before it is passed on to our visual cortices.[2] Less than half of what we see is actually based on information entering our eyes. The rest is pieced together out of our expectations of what the world should look like—in other words, from our inner images. As Talbot noted, "The eyes may be visual organs, but it is the brain that sees."[3] It is no exaggeration to say that we create our reality from our thoughts, beliefs, and the inner image programs we hold in our minds.

Our inner images have been shown to be capable of regulating blood flow, raising and lowering skin temperature, decreasing external bleeding, controlling heart rate, affecting blood pressure, increasing immune response, and increasing sexual arousal.[4] In addition, there is evidence that we can make things happen in the outside world simply by thinking them and holding an image of the desired result. As discussed in chapter 3, the work of Robert Jahn, head of the Princeton Engineering Anomalies Research group, showed that our thoughts can influence the output of machines simply by willing the output to happen. Science is beginning to support the notion that thoughts and images are "things" and have the ability to affect us and the world around us.

That thoughts and images have the ability to affect our world is an ancient belief that our Western, technological culture is just now beginning to rediscover. The roots go back thousands of years. The yogis of India believe that the world is nothing but an objectified dream and "whatever your powerful mind believes very intensely instantly comes to pass."[5] Similarly, the Persian mystics of the twelfth century believed that the world is created out of the subtle matter of thought, which they called *alam almithal*.[6] The tantric mystics of Tibet also held that thoughts were real things. They called the stuff of thoughts *tsal* and taught that every mental action produced waves of this invisible energy.[7] In other words, our thoughts and images have energy. This energy is like subtle matter, a higher vibration or frequency that is a precursor to the manifestation of the denser reality of the world we see around us. Our inner images and thoughts not only *affect* the world around us, but also in some more fundamental way they *create* it. If this is true, it is important for us to become aware of the image programs that are affecting us and begin to work with them at a conscious level. To do this is to live vibrantly and fully. Lacking this awareness, it is easy to become victims of a life that happens *to* us, a mindset that spawns the survival of the fittest, competitive approach so common in business today.

The notion that thoughts are things is an exciting intellectual concept. It is likely to stay only that unless you begin to experience it, embody it, and begin to work with it. When you do, it is dramatic and memorable. It can change your life forever. For instance, I [John] still remember the first time I actually experienced, in real time, my thoughts actually affecting the outer world around me:

I was on my way to work in the spring of 1981. It was a beautiful Chattanooga morning with a clear blue sky and billowing white clouds in the sky. I was sitting at a long traffic light thinking about something I'd read about—being able to melt clouds simply by thinking them away. I decided to try it. I picked out a small, wispy cloud and began to imagine nothing but blue sky in its place. I also began consciously to send thought energy to melt it. To my shock and amazement, the cloud disappeared in a matter of thirty seconds! I thought maybe I was crazy. So, throughout the rest of the day, I repeated the experiment with the same startling results. In my excitement, I taught my young children to do it too. We even used to have races to see who could melt clouds the fastest!

It's a simple demonstration of the power of the mind and one that can change the way you look at the world forever.

With the power that our inner images have, it is clear that we can spark more effective change in our lives by working with them consciously. Our thoughts are powerful, and our internal images are the natural language of the mind. Images communicate at deep levels beneath the ego consciousness. Working with our image programs to effect change in our lives is a very effective means of transforming our inner and outer reality.

Changing inner images to more positive ones is like rewriting our "software program" so we can lead more joyful, productive, healthy lives. This is because the subconscious mind does not differentiate images and input we receive from our physical senses from those that we create in our imagination. We can recruit the support of our subconscious minds if we intentionally form positive pictures or images in our minds. In our experience with this process, we have found that the result is both improvement in our outer reality and an almost limitless supply of energy. This is not a new discovery. Psychotherapists have recognized the transformative power of images at least since the early 1900s.

In the 1920s, Carl Happich, a German doctor, had his patients repeat a visualization until they were able to eliminate negative symbols and experience positive symbols in their place. He also had patients meditate on mandala-like designs to promote "spiritual integration."[8] In France, Caslant and Desoille worked with individuals to guide them through symbolic descent and ascent in the imaginal world to promote encounters with archetypal symbols of a mystical nature. In Switzerland, Gillerey "emphasized the neuromuscular correlates of mental imagery, believing that the resolution of conflicts at the imaginal level had a harmonizing physiological effect."[9] These researchers were not alone. Many others working with guided imagery followed in their path. The point is that science has recognized for some time that as inner images change, there is a corresponding shift on an outer level, including physiological changes. This is why visualization is now widely used to enhance performance in sports and business, accelerate learning, and promote healing (see chapter 4). We can apply this knowledge to make practical changes in our personal and professional life. Using energy symbols can make working with imagery even more powerful and effective.

In this chapter we explain what energy symbols are, why they work, in light of the science behind imagery discussed in chapter 3, and how to use these symbols to bring a greater sense of fulfillment and happiness into your life. We also give you examples of how we have used energy symbols and some exercises, so you can see for yourself how they work.

WHAT ARE ENERGY SYMBOLS?

In chapters 3 and 5 we mentioned archetypes in the collective unconscious as one contribution of Jungian psychology to the field of imagery. Another term for *archetypes* is *energy symbols.* As symbols, these special images are representations of something that can never be fully known, that are beyond complete understanding.[10] This class of images is universal, that is, energy symbols are found in all cultures and throughout all periods of history. They are more than simple pictures or signs and more than ordinary images, because when contemplated they have a profound impact on both mind and body. On more subtle energy levels, they also have a positive, enhancing effect on the soul.[11] They are *psychoenergetic*, invested with power on both mental and soul levels, and able to affect us physically. For example, the Tibetan monks have used psychoenergetic symbols in their meditative practices to help align and balance the *chakras*, the energy vortices associated with the endocrine glands in our bodies.[12]

Some of the most familiar images are energy symbols. We list some of them in Table 9.1 and include an ancient symbol from tantric yoga.

Table 9.1   Energy Symbols

 The infinity symbol has been associated for thousands of years with both infinite potential and perfect balance. It also stands for the power of transformation.

 A universal symbol from the remotest of times, the cross is pre-Christian. It symbolizes the meeting of heaven and earth, the Tree of Life, and archetypal man, the man who is capable of infinite and harmonious expansion on both the horizontal-earth and vertical-spiritual planes.[13]

 The circle is a widely used symbol for God, the Higher Self, completeness, and wholeness.

 This ancient symbol from tantric yoga is used in meditation by Tibetan monks to balance and align the energy centers in the body as they chant its name, "EEM."

 The medicine wheel is a Native American symbol for the wheel of life. The cross forms the spokes of the wheel, which gather and radiate energy from the four directions. It is also a metaphor for the psyche with mental (E), emotional (S), physical (W), and spiritual (N) components.

(Continued)

Table 9.1 Energy Symbols *(continued)*

	The sun represents God, life, essential fire and spirit, the Self (in the Jungian sense of the divine inner being), the hero, and masculine energy.
	The symbol of light stands for enlightenment, purity, goodness, wholeness, healing, truth, and the source of goodness, the manifestation of divinity, illumination, and direct knowledge. It brings with it the energy of enlightened beings such as the Christ and the Christ consciousness.
	The moon symbolizes fertility, night, duality, and the feminine.
	The egg represents immortality, fecundity (as in the Easter bunny), and, as the "cosmic egg," the world and space.
	Fish represent the life force, sacrifice, and the spiritual world.
	Mountains symbolize the spirit and the sacred joining of Heaven and Earth.
	Purification, transformation, and energy are associated with the element of fire.
	Nurturance, stability, and the feminine are meanings associated with the element of earth.
	Air symbolizes the intellect, thought, and change.
	Fluidity, healing, and feelings and emotions are some of the meanings of water. The ocean stands for universal life, the collective unconscious, and the sum of all possibilities.
	Birds, doves in particular, represent the spirit, creativity, and peace.

Many other energy symbols can be found in the references we cite in Appendix 3.

WHY DO ENERGY SYMBOLS WORK?

Energy symbols are familiar. You have probably seen every one of the symbols in the table. If they are familiar, they are also ancient. Their effects on body and mind have been well documented and observed over thousands of years by peoples as diverse as the Egyptians, Persians, Indians (both Eastern and American), and Chinese. If the prehistoric cave paintings of Europe are to be believed, human beings have been using the power of images to affect their lives and physical reality since the beginning of time. It is only in the last thirty years, however, that we have come to understand the effect of energy symbols on the brain.

In chapter 3 we review the scientific background of imagery. We mention there the work of David Bohm, a physicist and student of Einstein, who developed the concept of a holographic universe, a universe that transcends space and time. Bohm's work sparked Dr. Karl Pribram to take up the idea of holography as the model for brain functioning. In Pribram's view, the brain is a holographic storage device, any part of which contains the whole.[14] In this schema, images are frequencies of light energy with the property of holograms, which the brain interprets to construct concrete reality. Being holograms, the images in our minds come from a more fundamental primary holographic reality—the reality Bohm postulates as being beneath concrete reality as the *enfolded order.* As a result, when we work with images, we immerse ourselves in a reciprocal, reversible process that involves both the physical object and the image. When we make changes in outer, physical reality, our inner images change, and vice versa: *When we make changes in our inner images, we change physical reality.*

It is not only in the biological sciences that these insights have occurred. Many researchers—in art,[15] mythology,[16] comparative religion,[17] and psychology[18]—have observed the potency of images and how dozens of widely separated cultures have shared the same cluster of energy symbols. How can this be? Rupert Sheldrake hypothesized that it is the effect of the morphogenetic field—that human beings over time create a formative energy field that transcends centuries, cultures, and generations to create a powerful resonance in the psyche to which we respond.[19] The accumulated thought energy given to these images by millions of people comes to be stored in what Carl Jung called the *collective unconscious.* In our dreams, when we sleep, and in our imagery, when we use intuitive imagery, we touch into this oceanic reservoir of power and wisdom. If we apply energy symbols to our imagery, we can tap into the power they hold and use this power to change our outer reality.

WHEN AND WHERE TO USE ENERGY SYMBOLS

You can use energy symbols any time, but we have found them particularly useful in the following four situations:

- When you want more clarity in the images you are receiving as you use the intuitive imagery process (light is a particularly potent energy symbol for gaining more clarity)
- When you wish to create a more positive outcome than your imagery is suggesting you will obtain
- When you want to transform a situation or condition
- When you want to effect healing on the physical or spiritual level

Energy symbols can be used with both types of intuitive imagery—solo and partnered. In either case you must keep the process blind, so that the real question, or intuitive key, remains unknown. When you work with a partner, you can use energy symbols in the following situations:

- The imagery that your partner is receiving is unclear.
- Your partner is having difficulty receiving images.
- Your partner is nervous or anxious.

Whether you work alone or with a partner, it is not necessary that you understand the meaning, importance, or power of the symbol. It still creates an appropriate, effective response, according to your intention to do so.

HOW TO USE ENERGY SYMBOLS

The process of using energy symbols is simple, and the format is the same regardless of which energy symbol you choose. You send to the image you received doing intuitive imagery one of the energy symbols and see what happens to the original image. Use the guide instruction: "Send the image . . . [fill in the energy symbol you choose]. Describe what happens."

Here are the steps in the process:

Step 1: Choose a situation, event, or area in your life you wish to change for the better.

Step 2: Use the intuitive imagery process to receive an image of this situation, event, or area in your life as it is now. Record this image being careful to keep the process blind (if you are working solo, don't turn over the card).

Step 3: Choose the energy symbol that has the most power for you. With your imagination, send this symbol to the imagery you received. Trust that a transformation will occur. For example, you say, "Send the image light. Describe what happens."

Step 4: Record the results. How did the image change? How do you feel about the image now? How did you find the energy symbol worked for you?

Step 5: Look at the Intuitive Key and interpret both your original image and the image that appeared under the influence of the energy symbol.

Step 6: Apply the results. Work with the issue and your images in a conscious way to produce further changes.

Remember that the process is dynamic and reciprocal. As you create changes in your inner image reality, you will bring about changes in inner programming that then can transform your outer reality. Then you can do more imagery, from your new vantage point, to produce further change. Using energy symbols adds power to the transformative process and speeds it up.

Here is an example from our files:

A woman in mid-life wanted to gain insights into her life. She posed the question in intuitive imagery, "What does my life look like now?" Her prompt was, "Open a door and describe what you see." She received an image of a desert: a flat, barren, dry, hot place with nothing but desiccated earth and sand. There was nothing vertical at all in this landscape. It seemed a real hellhole, with no sign of life or movement. Overall, it was a most unappealing image. Then the woman decided to send this desert scene the energy symbol of light. Thereupon things began to move. She saw that her inner desert was not lifeless. She chose another energy symbol, water. After that image was sent to the original image, a great transformation occurred. The desert bloomed; there was green everywhere; things began to grow, first grass, then plants and bushes, and finally trees. At this point the woman stopped imaging and turned over the index card to reveal the subject of her imagery. When she saw that it was an image of her life, she realized that she needed to bring to her life healing, fluidity and flexibility, and deeper emotional expression—all qualities associated with water.

Exercise: Working with Energy Symbols for Transformation

1. Choose a situation, event, or area in your life that you want to change for the better.

2. Use the intuitive imagery process to receive an image of your choice, as it is now. Refer to chapters 6 and 7 if you need to refresh your memory on the basic process. Record your initial image here:

_____

_____

_____

_____

_____

3. Choose the energy symbol that holds the most power for you. You can choose from Table 9.1 or use another. In your imagination, send this symbol to the image you received in Step 2, knowing that a transformation will occur. Be sure to keep the process blind; don't look at the intuitive key.

4. What happened to the image? How did it change? How do you feel about it? Record your new image and feelings here:

_____

_____

_____

_____

5. What was your experience in working with the energy symbol?

_____

_____

_____

_____

6. Look at the intuitive key and interpret the images you received in Steps 2 and 3:

_____

_____

_____

_____

7. Begin to work with the issue and your images with the intention to make further changes. In other words, once you have the initial images, you can begin to work with them on a conscious level to make changes. Remember, as you are able to change your inner image reality, you make changes in the inner programming that then transforms your outer reality. Using energy symbols adds power to this transformation and can speed up the process.

NOTES

1. Sheikh and Kunzendorf 1984, 95–138.
2. Talbot 1991, 163.
3. Ibid.
4. Sheikh 1989, 34–40.
5. Yogananda 1973, 134.
6. Ibid., 260.
7. Talbot 1991, 221.
8. Crampton, Martha, *An Historical Survey of Mental Techniques in Psychotherapy and Description of the Dialogic Imagery Method* (self-published), 2.
9. Ibid., 4.
10. Hopcke 1989, 29.
11. Rodriguez, M., personal communication, 1989.
12. Faidych, personal communication, 1995. Evgueni Faidych is a physicist who has studied with the Dalai Lama.
13. Cooper 1978, 45.
14. Wolf 1984, 154–155.
15. E.g., Didron 1965.
16. E.g., Campbell 1949; Campbell 1976; Kerényi 1976; Eliade 1960.
17. Smith 1991.
18. Jung's *Collected Works*, especially volumes 9, 12, and 18; Jacobi 1959; Adler 1961; Jung et al. 1961.
19. Sheldrake 1981, 13.

10

Obstacles and How to Handle Them

The stuff of the universe is mind-stuff.

astronomer Arthur Eddington

Intuitive imaging is simple and easy to use, but this does not mean that things can't go wrong. In our experience teaching intuitive imagery to many people, we have seen several common types of problems. We identify these problem areas and offer possible causes and remedies for them in Table 10.1.

Many of the above trouble spots can be avoided by means of a careful following of the steps delineated in chapters 5 through 8. We have included single-page guidelines for doing intuitive imagery in Appendices 5 and 6, if you would like a handy reference to use during the process.

The best remedy for these and other types of problems is practice. Only with practice will you come to recognize your own unique style of imaging and the prompts that work best for you (and those that don't). Practice will also give you fluency in translating your unique imagery language and will build your sense of trust in yourself and the process. Be patient, and know that it *does* work, and that you *can* do it!

Table 10.1 Common Problems and Possible Remedies

Problem	Possible causes	Remedy
I can't get any images	A poorly defined question; a poorly worded question; lack of clarity about your goal; unconscious resistance to knowing the answer; taking multiple questions at once (i.e., holding all the cards in hand at the same time); no prompt or a poor choice of prompt; being too tense, nervous, or anxious; doing the imaging under a time constraint (trying to rush it).	Clarify your goal and question; determine whether you *really* want an answer; take one question/card at a time; use an appropriate prompt question; relax and give the process adequate time; you may be auditory or kinesthetic as your dominant sense, so try receiving a message or write down feelings or impressions instead of receiving an image; just "make something up"; practice the exercises in Appendix 2.
Images come and go during the imaging process	Too tense or nervous; too tired to hold a mental focus or to pick up the energy in the question.	Do one or more of the relaxation exercises in Appendix 2; do the process another time, when you feel more rested.
Vague or fuzzy results	Asking a vague or fuzzy question; posing too general a question; asking a compound question; resistance to knowing the answer; not ready to have an answer. This may not be a sign of trouble, if you were asking a yes or no question; the lack of clarity may be indicating a negative answer.	Clarify your question; make your question specific; ask a single question; be sure you want to have an answer; check to see if the fuzziness might be a sign of a *no* answer to your question.

Problem	Possible causes	Remedy
Poor answer quality	Question was trivial or not meaningful or important to you.	Ask only questions of significance; check yourself. Were you expecting a certain type of answer? Perhaps prior expectations are distorting your evaluation (this may be a good, valid answer, but not what you anticipated).
I get conflicting images during the imaging process.	You may be second-guessing yourself or judging the initial image.	Turn off your left brain's "voice of judgment"; trust that your first images are OK.
Impossible to make sense of images	You may not be ready to know the answer; the prompt may be inappropriate for the question; preconceived ideas may be blocking you from seeing the meaning; you may not be open to the message; the contents of the imagery may be so new that your conscious mind may not be ready to deal with them; you may be trying to force the process of insight.	Review whether you are ready to know the answer; change the prompt question; try to be more open to new ideas; give up forcing and let go; give the imagery time to percolate in your mind; try getting information from another sense, e.g., get a message or write down your impressions or feelings; pretend you *know* what the image means; use your imagination to make up an interpretation.
Images seem to have ambiguous meanings.	The original question may be vague; you may have some unconscious ambiguity or inner conflict around the question or receiving the answer.	Clarify your question; examine your feelings about knowing the answer; clarify that you really want to have an answer.

(Continued)

Table 10.1 Common Problems and Possible Remedies *(continued)*

Problem	Possible causes	Remedy
Images are difficult to relate to the question.	Prompt may be inappropriate for the question.	Choose a new prompt (consult Table 7.1).
I received no new information or insights.	You may not be looking deeply enough; the image confirms what you already know; or you peeked at the question and the left brain took over.	Look at the image again to see what deeper meaning there is to discover; confirming images say you were right all along; stop peeking!
Decline in quality of imagery over the course of doing the imaging.	You may be trying to do too much imagery in one sitting.	Rest; have a change of scene or pace; do imagery in shorter intervals of time.
Widely divergent images in response to the same question (when doing imagery with a group of partners).	This may not necessarily be a sign of trouble; it may indicate a multiplicity of perspectives or divergent interests related to the question; there may be a common theme; or there may not be one single *best* alternative or answer at this time.	Make sure your question and intent are clear; look for a common underlying theme; do further imagery work focused on the areas of divergence to gain more insight; situations change over time, so repeat the imaging again at a later date.
Confusion or conflict among different books and experts about what my images mean.	You aren't trusting your own inner wisdom to reveal the image to you.	Ignore books and experts; rely on your own associations, meanings, and insights.

IV

Examples of the Use of Intuitive Imagery

11

Using Intuitive
Imagery in Daily Living

> Every feeling, thought, movement, and encounter is simultaneously an
> inner and outer event.
>
> *psychologist Arnold Mindell*

In this chapter and the next we offer some concrete examples of
how people have used intuitive imagery to address practical
problems in daily life and business. Because we want to illustrate
not only how the process is used but also what it actually looks
like, with all its components, we have reproduced each example
exactly as it was done, including the date, background, and results. We have changed only the names of individuals to protect
their privacy.

GAINING INSIGHT INTO PERSONAL ISSUES
WITH INTUITIVE IMAGERY

I [John] have worked with individuals using intuitive imagery to
gain deeper insight into personal issues and health problems.
One woman told me that imagery got her to the same place in
twenty minutes that it took her two years in therapy to achieve.
This is not to discredit traditional talking therapies. However, it

does demonstrate the power of using this kind of imagery for therapeutic purposes. The following example illustrates how imagery can be used to uncover deep personal issues, in this case, resulting from a childhood experience of sexual abuse.

Date: February 23, 1993

Intuitive Key: Something That Represents or Symbolizes Your Back Pain

Guide: See an image. What do you see?

Image: I'm at the bottom of the stairs. I felt really anxious going down them. I'm in the basement. It's dark.

Interpretation: Going down the stairs is a metaphor for going down the spine to the lower back area. Also, Donna was sexually abused as a very young child by her uncle. This may have occurred in the basement setting seen in the image. So there is an almost immediate connection between her lower back pain and her early childhood. Low back pain often symbolizes support issues.

Intuitive Key: What Do You Know about This Basement That Connects with Your Back Pain?

Guide: Merge with and become the darkness. What do you know?

Image: It's cold. Mildewed. I'm afraid. I'm getting a jabbing pain in my left ear . . . [pause] . . . it's gone now. I feel off balance.

Interpretation: The fear keeps her off balance, which may lead to spinal misalignments and pain.

Intuitive Key 3: A Story about the Connection to Your Back Pain

Guide: Tell me a story about where you are.

Image: I'm looking up at a door where there is light. It is too steep to get there. Now I feel cold and afraid. I feel paralyzed. I can't move any further. I know if I could just get around the back corner that there would be light; I'd go out into the sun. But I can't move!

Interpretation: Donna's fear has frozen something that is stored in her back. It is now surfacing. If she could just get around the back corner and release it, there would be healing.

Intuitive Key: A Person Who Represents Your Back Pain, the Root Problem

Guide: Meet a person. Whom do you see? What do you know about this person?

Image: An old man's face. . . . It's my uncle! Fat, plump, and a big nose. Almost bald with white hair. His face is wrinkly.

Interpretation: This is the uncle that sexually abused Donna when she was less than three years old. The image confirms that the back pain is connected somehow with this early incident.

Intuitive Key: Something That Makes You Feel Better, a Cure

Guide: This person gives you something. What is it?

Image: He doesn't give me anything. I hate him! He won't let me go. He makes me stay on his lap. He wants to play with me. He pinches me.

Interpretation: Donna needs to process all the anger and fear from the abuse incident to cure her back pain.

Intuitive Key: Something That Makes You Feel Better, a Cure

Guide: Imagine something magical. Merge with it and tell me what you know.

Image: A big marble with colors all swirled inside. When I merge with it, I feel fluid and vibrant.

Interpretation: The marble is a symbol of wholeness. Donna will experience wholeness and vibrancy when she allows her fluid, feminine side to fully express the swirl of her emotions.

USING INTUITIVE IMAGERY TO UNDERSTAND HEALTH PROBLEMS

In this example, "Jan," or the person we will call Jan, had persistent back problems. In dealing with this kind of situation, it is often helpful first to get some general information about the person, so we began with general questions and then took up the health concern.

Date: March 10, 1994

Intuitive Key: A Person Who Represents Jan Walters

Guide: See a person and describe him or her. What qualities does he or she have?

Image: I'm having a hard time seeing a person. I see a faceless, sexless person wearing jeans and a brushed denim shirt. I'm looking at the person from the back. This person is strong, yet gentle, likes animals a lot, is trustworthy, has been around horses. The person has an accent, but I'm not sure what type.

Interpretation: The image hints that you don't value yourself enough. You have a hard time seeing yourself as a whole person. Yet you pick up on your strong character virtues of strength, gentleness, love of animals (especially horses), and trustworthiness.

Intuitive Key: Why Is Jan So Hard on Herself?

Guide: Tell me a brief story about this person.

Image: The person has dirt on his or her hands. The person has been digging for worms in the compost pile (that is, the horse manure). The person is going to go fishing. The sky is bright blue. The sun is reflecting off everything. I see fish in the water. It is late spring or early summer. Fishing is the perfect thing.

Intuitive Key: Three Things That Represent Jan's Reward for Her Hard Work

Guide: Find three things. What do you see?

Image: (1) A tackle box; (2) a fishing rod; (3) paper towel to wipe the dirt off my hands

Interpretation: You have gone through a period of digging in the "compost" both in your personal journey and in your business. The image suggests that it may be time to recognize that the sun is shining. Things will be looking up. Now is the time to reward yourself. Wipe the dirt off your hands and go fishing. Begin valuing yourself for the progress you've made.

Intuitive Key: Something That Reveals Why Jan Sometimes Has Self-destructive Tendencies

Guide: Imagine something this person is doing. What is it?

Image: I see myself on a horse riding in the woods on a trail, looking at things you don't normally look at.

Interpretation: Spending rejuvenating time riding in the woods is something you don't normally do. If you will take time to do more things to value yourself, you will find that your business and personal life will prosper as well. That's because they'll reflect the greater value you have for yourself.

Intuitive Key: A Structure That Represents Jan's Back Problems

Guide: Imagine a structure and tell me a brief story about it. What kind of shape is the structure in?

Image: It is a pick-up truck. There are a couple of bales of hay in the back. It is old and beat up, in pretty bad shape, but fairly dependable. It blew out on a curve, though.

Guide: Tell me what you know about the truck. What does it need from you?

Image: The truck doesn't like Jan driving it. It needs respect. It wants me to understand that it is older and did OK in its day.

Interpretation: The truck became a perfect metaphor for your back, which doesn't like the way you drive it. The back, as we discussed, is often symbolic of support issues. You may feel as though you have been going through a tough time when you weren't supported or have faced fearful support (money) issues. What your back is asking you for is more respect, which might be read as more self-respect, valuing yourself more, taking more time for yourself.

USING INTUITIVE IMAGERY TO GAIN INSIGHT INTO A CHILD WITH PROBLEMS

Sometimes our children can present us with real dilemmas, making us feel like we need the wisdom of Solomon to know what to do and how best to meet their needs. Intuitive imagery can put you in touch with that wisdom, as the following example illustrates.

The mother of a teenage boy with recurring drug and school problems used intuitive imagery to gain insights into what was going on and what he needed. Note the use of the energy symbol (light) in the second guide prompt.

Date: July 24, 1994

Intuitive Key: An Image of Andrew (the Son) and What Is Going on with Him

Guide: See a structure. Describe it and what is going on there.

Image: I see this sculpture covered with a lot of what looks to me like a clay formation all over.

Interpretation: This is how Andrew's mother sees him—like a stone figure and encrusted with a surface substance that is hiding his beauty.

Guide: Now put light on this scene. What happens?

Image: I see a lot of people chiseling at the sculpture in order to make its beauty visible again. I can see part of the feet and shoes only.

Interpretation: It's likely that Andrew's transformation would entail some "chiseling" at his surface persona on the part of many people. His mother may not have been able at the time to see the whole picture, but she got a basic or fundamental (feet) sense of what was needed.

Result: With the support of his family, this young man enrolled in a high school that emphasized building character values over academic achievement. It turned out that both son and mother experienced a "chiseling" process, which revealed the beauty of both over time.

USING INTUITIVE IMAGERY TO MAKE A MAJOR DECISION

When you are at an important choice point in life, intuitive imagery can be a very useful tool in helping to sort out what to do.

A man we will call Henry confronted such a point in the fall of 1995. He knew he wanted to divorce his wife, but he lived in New York, and from all he had heard about its antiquated divorce laws, he sensed he would not be able to afford the legal process. He investigated alternatives and learned that both Nevada and Alaska had simpler procedures. What should he do? At this point, he turned to intuitive imagery.

Date: October 1, 1995

Intuitive Key: The Three Choices Facing Henry Around His Divorce

Door 1 = going to Nevada for the divorce; *Door 2* = getting the divorce in New York; *Door 3* = going to Alaska for the divorce

Guide: See three doors. Describe each.

Image: Door 1 is very plain, just a door, no trim or decoration, an average door. Door 2 is very fancy, with fine moldings and gilt trim. Door 3 is a big, old, solid wooden door, with iron straps and big square nailheads. It looks like the door to a castle.

Intuitive Key: What Henry Might Expect in Each of His Three Options

Guide: Open each door and describe what you see.

Image: I open Door 1 and see an empty room. There is nothing there. I leave. Door 2 opens to a beautiful living room with Louis XV furniture and crystal chandeliers and wall sconces and a big table with a white tablecloth piled high with fancy foods. It is very opulent. I feel out of place. It is too rich for my blood. I don't belong here. I go to the third door. It is very strong. I open it; it swings easily and reveals a big room, all of stone, very strong, with thick walls. It is cold in this room, but I feel safe and secure here.

Intuitive Key: Identify Which State Henry Should Use for His Divorce

Guide: Which of the three doors and rooms appeals to you most?

Image: The third, the door to the castle.

Interpretation: Henry's intuition picked up on his earlier sense that the New York divorce might be too costly. In the imagery he knew he did not belong there. Interestingly, the imagery also got the sense of Alaska, that going there in winter would be cold, as the castle room was cold.

Result: Henry did go to Alaska, based on this guidance, and his divorce was speedy, efficient, and a tiny fraction of the cost of a New York legal proceeding.

USING INTUITIVE IMAGERY TO CLARIFY LIFE PURPOSE AND VOCATION

In this example a very successful marketer, whom we will call Grace, used intuitive imagery to get a new sense of direction for her life. She had come to feel she had done enough in the area of marketing and corporate communications and felt there was something more, some greater purpose for her life.

Date: July 16, 1995

Intuitive Key: A Person That Symbolizes Grace's Purpose in Life

Guide: Meet a person.

Image: I see a woman, perhaps in her fifties or sixties, who runs a small motel in Seal Beach, California. There are red and white checked tablecloths in the restaurant on the lower floor, and she absolutely delights in sharing her little piece of the world with visitors. She enjoys making things out of shells and other natural materials and feels that she can help people get in touch a little bit more with nature from her crafts, which she sells and often gives away. She is married to a bald man, and they are content. Things are fairly simple in their world, but they feel that they have a true divine purpose in sharing it with all the visitors that come to stay with them.

Intuitive Key: The Career Options Grace Is Considering

Door 1 = keep doing what she has been doing; *Door 2* = a path in the healing arts; *Door 3* = work in sales

Guide: See three doors.

Image: Behind Door 1 I see an American dream suburban scene with kids playing in a cul-de-sac, a station wagon in a driveway, and an ice cream truck. This is not a comfortable scene for me. Behind Door 2 I see Kenya—sweeping warm, yellow plains with Kilimanjaro rising in the background. Everything has a solar earth glow about it. It feels wholesome, spiritual, and deeply connected with the earth. Door 3 opens into a Victorian parlor, with fringed lampshades and red velvet chairs. It feels very traditional and also familiar to me. But I feel that people come there to discuss topics that I have already been over a hundred times, and as pleasant as it is, there isn't much for me to learn there.

Guide: Go back to the woman running the hotel. In which of these three scenes—suburbia, Kenya, or the parlor—do you think she would prefer to take a vacation?

Image: Kenya

Guide: In which scene would she most like to live?

Image: Kenya

Interpretation: A career path in the healing arts would hold the greatest appeal for Grace.

Result: The intuitive imagery session had a great impact on Grace, and she decided to leave marketing. This required that she relocate and take up formal learning of a whole new area of knowledge for her, so she could become a naturopathic physician.

CONCLUSION

These are just a handful of examples of people using intuitive imagery in daily life and decision-making. The circumstances can be portentous, as in the cases of Henry and Grace, or minor. We use intuitive imagery often to decide things like which movie to see and which restaurant to choose. Big or small, the choice points of life are easier and more supportive of our wholeness when handled intuitively. This is equally true for the choice points and decisions in the world of business, as we reveal in chapter 12.

12

Business Uses of Intuitive Imagery

You can't embrace the new paradigm until you let go of the old.

Marilyn Ferguson

Intuitive imagery is as useful in business as it is in daily living. In this chapter we provide a range of examples of how business people have put intuitive imagery to use to improve their businesses, in both internal and external applications.

Some examples are from individual business people; others were conducted by a small cross-functional team I [John] put together while I was at DuPont. This team called itself the SWAT team, an acronym for special weapons and tactics. We shared a conviction that new approaches were needed to remain competitive in our businesses and that intuition could be harnessed for practical use. To test this, we used intuitive imagery in parallel with traditional analytical techniques, applying it to a broad spectrum of business issues. Over a three-year period, we found imaging to be a consistently reliable and reproducible way of accessing intuition. We were able not only to gain deeper insight into existing situations but also frequently to assess the future impact of a course of action. The imaging we did as a team was

145

not exclusive to DuPont, because the SWAT team occasionally did projects for outside groups.

In this chapter, we present some representative examples from a variety of business applications. As with the examples from daily life in chapter 11, the names of people and companies have been changed to maintain confidentiality and protect individual privacy. In some examples, those doing imagery have been designated with numbers, such as Imager 1 and Imager 2.

INTUITIVE IMAGERY IN THE INTERNAL BUSINESS ENVIRONMENT

The following examples are just a few of the many ways managers can use intuitive imagery to define, guide, direct, and improve the internal operations of their businesses.

Identifying Core Strengths and Priorities

One of the key challenges facing corporate leaders these days is getting an accurate answer to the questions, What business are we in? and What are our core strengths and priorities? Here are some excerpts from a large imagery exercise that illustrate how intuitive imagery was used to help a large urban holistic learning center answer these questions. This also demonstrates how group imaging is handled to arrive at a consensus answer.

Date: August 13, 1990

Intuitive Key: What Are the Key Strengths of This Learning Center?

1 = the unique role of this center in its community; 2 = the staff; 3 = the building; 4 = the center's future vision; 5 = the bookstore; 6 = the catalogue; 7 = the programming and teachers; 8 = the scholarship and volunteer program; 9 = the founder

Guide: Imagine you are playing the celebrity stars tic-tactoe game with the boxes numbered 1 through 9. Which number or numbers light up first?

Imager 1: Numbers 3, 5, and 7 light up

Imager 2: Numbers 7, 5, and 3 light up

Imager 3: Numbers 5, 7, and 9

Imager 4: Numbers 5 and 8

Imager 5: Numbers 3 and 4 light up

Interpretation: There is a consensus among the imagers that the bookstore is the center's key strength. Three of five also agree that the programming and the building are core strengths.

Intuitive Key: What Is the Most Important Area to Emphasize?

1 = increase revenues; 2 = contain costs

Guide: Imagine two boxes, box 1 and box 2. Which box is larger or are you drawn to first? Look inside the box and describe what you find.

Imager 1: Box 1 is larger. Inside is a Muppet snake with big eyes. He says, "I represent knowledge, rebirth, and playfulness."

Imager 2: Box 1 is larger. Inside it are protective straw and a very thin crystalline ornament.

Imager 3: Box 1 is a large, plain, white box. Inside is a valuable doll that is in need of repair.

Imager 4: Box 1 is larger. It has lots of kids' games and toys, brightly colored and fun.

Imager 5: Box 2 is larger. Inside are old manuscripts and letters describing experiences and travels of an unknown relative in a land far away.

Interpretation: It is more important to concentrate on increasing revenues short-term than on containing costs, probably because it is quicker. There is also something about a spirit of playfulness and fun that will attract greater revenues.

Intuitive Key: Where Is the Best Area to Focus on for Increased Revenues?

1 = registration; 2 = bookstore; 3 = memberships; 4 = contributions

Guide: Imagine four buildings side by side numbered 1 through 4. What is the relative size of each building on a scale of 1 to 10, 10 being the largest? Describe each and tell what you know about the structure.

Imager	Largest (4 points)	Second (3 points)	Third (2 points)	Smallest (1 point)
1	2, a new high rise with lots of energy and high spirits	3, a traditional office building	4, a vacation house in the tropics with servants	1, old, dusty, and run down
2	4, a space station supporting a city and ecosystem	2, a hoverport for landing spacecraft	1, small building on earth	3, a house that will be blasted away for new development
3	4, a large brick house, friendly and inviting	3, a large frame house	2, the house in front of the garage	1, a small garage
4	4, futuristic; this is where dreaming takes place; the building of tomorrow	3, where all present projects are worked on; very busy	2, all past history is kept here; lots of journals and pictures	1, an entrance building; it keeps track of the people who have been in and out of the other buildings
5	1, a skyscraper; the world's tallest building	3, office building overlooking a lake; beautiful view	4, a condominium; people own and pay for maintenance and security; well kept	2, a multistory residence; houses several families, all struggling to find their way

Imager Largest (4 points)	*Second (3 points)*	*Third (2 points)*	*Smallest (1 point)*
Overall rating			
4 = contribu-tions	3 = member-ships	2 = bookstore	1 = registra-tion

Interpretation: The strongest consensus is around contributions as the best way to improve revenues in the short run, and perhaps for achieving dreams of the future (Imager 4). Implementing a restructured membership program is second in priority. Not to be dismissed is the potential for improving revenues from the bookstore.

Results: Contributions did turn out to be the largest area of increased revenues over the next two years.

Clarifying Team Purpose

Another important component of successful business performance these days is effective teamwork, which depends on a shared clarity of purpose. Intuitive imagery can be useful here, as illustrated by the following example of solo imagery done to clarify the purpose of a team of four managers given the responsibility to make a group of forty-four employees more cohesive and, simultaneously, more flexible.

Date: March 12, 1989

Intuitive Key: An Image of the Purpose of the Technical Service and Development Management Team

Guide: Open a door. What do you find?

Image: A close-up image of a black strap with a gray buckle fastener, much like the strap and fastener on a book bag. Then the image shifts to ballet dancers, four of them. They all wore matching costumes and were dancing in perfect synchronization.

Interpretation: The strap and fastener meant to band together tightly. The four dancers (managers) need to coordinate efforts so they can be in perfect synchronization and harmony. Dance is a feminine symbol of emotional expression of inner feelings. A caring approach by the managers is indicated. (Note how the image picked up on the fact there were four managers [dancers] even though the imaging was blind.)

Results: The management team did bond tightly, closely coordinated its efforts, and managed with a participatory and empowering style. The results were an impressive increase in group productivity.

Planning for Meetings and Presentations

A major component of business success is solid preparation. Intuitive imagery can be used to anticipate what's coming, for example, to plan realistically for meetings and presentations to any group, including a sales team, higher management, or a board of directors. Here is one example of how the use of intuitive imagery helped a business manager prepare for a presentation to a regional sales group. Note how the imagery led the manager to anticipate resistance and a time of scrutiny for his group's new direction. This allowed him to react with composure and transform the outcome.

Date: March 8, 1989

Intuitive Key: How Will the Presentation on the Future Direction of the Technical Organization Be Received by the Eastern Sales Group?

Guide: Open a door. What do you find?

Image: I found myself looking up like a patient on an operating room table. Above me was a huge round surgical light.

There were onlookers peering down at me over the edge of a balcony that circled the entire room.

Interpretation: There will be lots of intense interest and scrutiny. The presenter will be much like a patient on an operating table.

Result: At the meeting, the technical manager did find himself under a good deal of scrutiny, like being under the surgical light in the image. He encountered skepticism about aspects of the new direction his group was taking. There were lots of questions from the director of sales, regional sales manager, marketing manager, product manager, and sales people—the entire gallery of people seen in the image. Yet the technical manager was able to react with composure because he had been forewarned by the image.

Intuitive Key: What Concerns Will the Sales Group Have About the Technical Group's Future Direction?

Guide: Meet someone.

Image: A man wearing a swimmer's cap standing waist-deep in the snow struggling to maintain control over a large, powerful chain saw. He is afraid that he is going to lose control, and the chain saw will injure him.

Interpretation: The man in the snow represents sales. He is standing out in the cold, struggling to maintain control over a chain saw (the technical group) which just might cut him badly. Sales is concerned about losing control over the technical organization.

Result: The concerns of the sales group were justified. The technical organization was being asked to take more of a leadership role and step up to the plate as a full partner. The image clearly showed that this would be a source of concern for sales. It would take time for them to understand and adjust.

Intuitive Key: What Will the Relationship with the Sales Group Be After the Presentation?

Guide: Open another door. What do you find?

Image: I am looking down a long hall. At the end of it, a goldfish bowl sits atop a stand. The bowl has electric blue water in it, radiating a soft light.

Interpretation: The technical organization will be under scrutiny, as if they were in a fishbowl. The color blue is associated with communication. The image implies that the way to overcome the resistance that will be encountered is to communicate with the sales organization.

Result: The technical manager made communication with sales a high priority. Over the year following his presentation, the sales group and technical group became full partners, both in serving customers in the marketplace and in developing new products.

Handling Human Resources Issues

Intuitive imagery is very successful in helping managers understand the deeper needs of the people in their group. This is particularly effective in understanding the development needs of people and getting to the root causes of personnel problems that arise. To illustrate this second point, I [John] have chosen a poignant example from my own experience as a manager. This example uses intuitive imagery to identify an employee's needs and motivations. It concerns a black woman in her early thirties whom I will call Reann who was transferred into my technical group in 1990. She had a master's degree in chemical engineering and a background in research in which she was not treated well by her previous managers. She was looking to catch up on what she felt was lost time in her career. After a brief time in the group, she asked for a transfer to California to become part of a plant technical organization. The real (undisclosed) motivating factor behind this was family on the West Coast.

Date: **May 13, 1990**

Intuitive Keys

a. A person that symbolizes Reann

b. More information about Reann

c. Will she be successfully transferred to California in the next three months?

Guides

a. See a person and describe. Give strengths and weaknesses.

b. See a structure.

c. Mentally snap your fingers. What happens to the person and structure now? Get a message.

Images

a. An image of a firebird. He is like the symbol of the United States with the eagle holding the arrows. But he is landing in a cloud of smoke from his rocket thrusters. At first, he has a space helmet on. *Strengths:* The firebird is powerful and brings insights from his journeys to other worlds. *Weaknesses:* He has developed a certain amount of pride and aloofness.

b. As a structure, I see a powerful rocket ship blasting off. Its course has been set, yet the rocket has a mind of its own. It will make course corrections under its own control once free of the Earth's gravitational pull. Its purpose is to bring back knowledge of other worlds.

c. The firebird is being shot at. He is in danger and is afraid. All pride is gone under fire. He quickly dons his space helmet to take off for outer space, but his helmet has been damaged. He is stuck. *Message:* Don't be so sure of yourself, for others will pull you up short.

Interpretations

a. The image of the firebird landing in a cloud of smoke, clenching arrows in his talons is simultaneously an image of power and of anger. The helmet covers his true face. Something is not being spoken. Reann brings the strength of her technical knowledge and the diversity of her background into the group. Yet she also brings pride and aloofness that present obstacles in working as a team player.

b. The rocket ship image hints at Reann's desire to leave the company.

c. The transfer is not likely to happen in the next three months. This is likely to increase Reann's desire to leave the company (take off for outer space).

Result: For Reann to be successfully transferred, a job had to be specially created for her. We ultimately could not find a way to do this. So Reann actually did feel stuck. Despite efforts to move her into an assignment that offered a high profile and growth opportunities, she found a way to leave the company. She took a job on the West Coast with a competitor.

Prioritizing Tasks

Nobody we know in business has enough time to accomplish all the tasks on the "To Do" list. Life seems to be about making choices, especially at work. There is a universal need to learn how to set meaningful priorities. Intuitive imaging can slice through to underlying factors so that priorities take into account often hidden, unconscious needs. The next example shows an effective, relatively quick process for prioritizing a list of emphasis areas common to managing a group with an industry-wide focus. Note the imaging framework. A general intuitive key, which provides an imaging focus, is used with a general guide prompt for an entire series of questions. It's an effective way to do solo imaging.

Date: **March 28, 1989**

General Intuitive Key: In which area is it important to concentrate efforts over the next six months for the success of the group and the greatest contribution to the business?

General Guide: See a musical instrument. Note its type and condition. Does it sound sweet or harsh? Does it need more practice?

Intuitive Key 1: New Product Planning and Development

Image 1: An old, upright piano that is in poor condition and out of tune. It needs some tender loving care, and more practice.

Intuitive Key 2: Establishing Industry Contacts

Image 2: A pair of shiny cymbals. They have just been struck, and a nice sound is radiating outward. They are in good condition and played often enough.

Intuitive Key 3: Quality—Total Quality Management (TQM)

Image 3: An oboe in fair to poor condition. There seems to be a restriction at the bottom end. The sound is OK, but the musician is straining to play it. Needs more practice.

Intuitive Key 4: Trade Associations and Conferences

Image 4: A tuba with an elongated top portion. It has a nice sound but is a bit high-pitched for a tuba. It is in good condition, but maybe needs to be toned down.

Intuitive Key 5: Coaching and Counseling

Image 5: An oboe in good condition. Beautiful sound. A nice balance with the rest of the orchestra.

Intuitive Key 6: Information Management

Image 6: A violin. There is a radiating light behind it. But the violin is worn, and in need of re-conditioning. It's broken, no strings!

Intuitive Key 7: Communication with Other Groups

Image 7: Long baroque horns, the kind with banners hanging from them. Fanfare. Bright and shiny. In good condition.

Intuitive Key 8: Group Recognition Awards

Image 8: A pipe organ with pipes tipped in gold. I hear a majestic cathedral sound from a virtuoso organist.

Intuitive Key 9: Stimulating Creativity and Innovation

Image 9: Tools instead of an instrument. First the scythe, then a pickax. They are new and haven't been used much.

Intuitive Key 10: Performance Appraisals

Image 10: A French horn in fairly good condition. It may need only slight touching up and a bit more practice.

Interpretation: High priority, tier 1 areas are information management (broken), new product planning and development (in bad shape), quality and TQM (poor condition, training needed, the organization is straining to play it). Stimulating creativity and innovation falls in the next tier of effort and is linked with new product development. Performance reviews need only modest effort and are tier 3. Efforts with trade associations need to be toned down, and the human resources committed to them focused elsewhere. Everything else is in pretty good shape.

Results: These became the priorities for a new manager who used them to get off to a fast start with a new group in a new industry.

INTUITIVE IMAGERY IN THE EXTERNAL BUSINESS ENVIRONMENT

Whether it is identifying customer needs or figuring the best way to acquire new business, intuitive imagery has myriad uses outside the walls of the corporation. Here are four examples.

Identifying Latent Customer Needs

Intuitive imagery is very effective at identifying latent customer needs. Our businesses are becoming more and more culturally and ethnically diverse. Imaging can be very effective in revealing not only latent product needs and hidden agendas but also in bringing into our awareness cultural needs to which we might be blind. This may be especially important in serving international markets.

Professional selling involves not only understanding customers' product needs but also their positional needs. The following excerpt from an imaging session shows how an experienced salesman received insight into the unspoken needs of the president and vice president of an important customer. This led him to sell at the right level and to strengthening of the selling relationship. In the example that follows, note how the images (which are, remember, done without knowing the keys) home in on the positional levels as well as the customer's needs.

Date: **August 10, 1989**

Intuitive Key: The President of the Widget Company

Guide: Meet person 1 and tell a story about him or her, including strengths and weaknesses.

Image: A king with a golden crown. He is middle aged with long, dark hair. His castle is not opulent, or wealthy. The king is not terribly happy. He would like to be more prosperous but doesn't quite know how to go about getting there. He is awaiting advice from his counselors and knights on how to improve the situation. *Strengths:* The king is pure of heart and has a desire to do well by his subjects. He has a thirst for knowledge and deep insight into the meanings of things. *Weaknesses:* The king lacks confidence and is not seen as a particularly strong leader. He is given to a certain moodiness and tendency toward pessimism. He needs to lighten up and not be so intense.

Interpretation: The president covers a lack of confidence with his intensity. He is a thinker with deep insight and a thirst for knowledge . . . probably has an analytical personality style. He wants to do well for his people. You can trust him.

Intuitive Key: How Does the President Feel About the Widget Company?

Guide: Person 1 finds something. How does he feel about it?

Image: He finds a magic sword, like Excalibur! It is shining in the darkness and radiates great power. He is awed by the sword's beauty and power, and his demeanor becomes more regal with it.

Interpretation: This image confirms the president's deep feeling for the company and its people. He has respect for the company.

Intuitive Key: How Can Burt Reach out to the President?

Guide: Person 1 makes a wish. What is it?

Image: The king wishes for wealth enough to distribute among the subjects of his kingdom. He wants to make their lives better. Yet he wants to be seen as a strong leader whose legacy is in achieving abundance for the kingdom. He also desires the respect and authority that such an accomplishment will bring.

Interpretation: The salesman can strengthen his relationship through partnering on the new distributor program to increase the Widget Company's profitability. He needs to be aware of the president's analytical style. He will want to know facts, figures, and details.

Intuitive Key: The Vice President of the Widget Company

Guide: Meet person 2 and tell a story about him or her, including strengths and weaknesses.

Image: Strange. This person is on horseback and is wearing kingly robes and a crown also. But I don't think this guy is really a king. His bearing and demeanor are much more regal than person 1. But he is riding and prancing around in circles within a courtyard. He is alone. The impression I get is that he is play-acting. He wants to be king. He has a very big ego. He is not yet king but feels he is the real power behind the throne.

Interpretation: The vice president has very big ego needs that must be respected for a relationship to work. He is a real "driver" who will expect ready answers, will expect a summary instead of a lot of facts, and will want the salesman's best shot at every meeting. While catering to the vice president's ego needs, it may be better to deal directly with the president for final decisions.

Intuitive Key: What Is the Relationship Between the Vice President and the President of the Widget Company?

Guide: Person 2 meets person 1. How do they feel about each other?

Image: When they meet, person 2 is no longer dressed as a king. Rather, he is a prominent knight of the kingdom. He kneels before person 1, who is the real king and a very intelligent man. The king recognizes his own weaknesses and feels he needs the strength of this knight to run the kingdom. He is, however, somewhat wary of the knight's motivations. The king is occasionally cowed by the strength of the knight.

Interpretation: The president recognizes the personal power of the vice president and uses it as an asset. But he is also wary of the vice president's motivations. It is important that the salesman be aware of this political power struggle but not get caught in the crossfire. Both men are motivated by increasing the revenues and profits of the Widget Company, but for different reasons. The president wants to be respected by his people and to make their lives better. The vice president wants to benefit personally.

Results: The imaging prepared the salesman for an important meeting with both the president and vice president to discuss a new distributor program. The salesman, who was skeptical of the imaging but open-minded enough to try it, was pleasantly surprised by the results of the effort. He sent the SWAT team the following comments after his meeting: "I am very happy to report that there was nothing inconsistent between the imaging work . . . and what transpired at the meeting. The black knight (vice president) appears to be much more open and friendly than would have been predicted but our assessment of his ambition and his relationship to the king (president) seems to be right on target. . . . I have concluded that having done the imaging I was better prepared for the meeting than if I had not done it. I will definitely want to use imaging again as a tool in my business relationships." Burt became a convert!

Evaluating the Impact of Possible Courses of Action

Intuitive imagery can be used to get some sense of what possible actions, like price increases, would have on the business. In the following example the imaging was done for a large polymers business. It clearly showed that a recent price increase was leading to weakness in the market and gains by the competition. Something needed to be done to recoup lost sales.

Date: June 21, 1989

Intuitive Key: An Image of the Business and a Description of its Current Strength in the Marketplace

Guide: Imagine a river. Describe its size, rate of flow, and any other prominent characteristics or surroundings that come to mind.

Image: Very green banks. The water is silver, silver-tinged. The river is wide, about a half-mile across. It carries a lot of water but doesn't flow very fast. It empties into a huge lake, as big as one of the Great Lakes.

Interpretation: The business is large, carrying a lot of volume and feeding into an even larger business of which it is a part. It is not seen as moving very fast.

Intuitive Key: The Impact of the Recent Price Increase

Guide: Mentally snap your fingers. What happens to the river and its flow rate?

Image: The silver tint is starting to disappear from the river, starting from the source where the water flows very fast. The river is being contaminated at the source, and the contamination is flowing down and polluting the whole river. The river hasn't become totally contaminated yet but is well on its way to becoming so.

Interpretation: The price increase has led to a slowdown in the market. It is contaminating the entire business. Something needs to be done.

Making a Pitch for New Business

Salesmanship is a key to success in business, and understanding customer needs is, in turn, the key to professional selling. Intuitive imagery can help identify customer needs, aid in the formulation of an effective sales presentation, and take much of the fear and uncertainty out of the initial sales call. In the following example an advertising executive wanted to gain the business of a large company outside his normal selling area and was going to have a meeting with its chief executive officer. He needed insight into the company, the chief executive officer, and how best to package his presentation.

Date: March 10, 1994

Intuitive Key: A Structure That Represents Jack Smith of the EVZ Company

Guide: See a structure and describe it.

Image: A little cabin in a field. It is like the one I see sometimes in a nightmare, where dolls inside have all been torn apart. But as I look inside, this cabin is clean. Nobody has been there in a while.

Interpretation: Your fear about meeting Jack Smith comes through in the image of the nightmare. But the cabin is seen not to be the same as in the nightmare. Instead it is clean and hasn't had anyone visit for a long time. You may find Jack Smith to be a fairly simple man (like the cabin) who will relish the attention you can bring him. He probably hasn't had anyone like you do his advertising for him in some time, if ever.

Intuitive Key: Something That Bill (Imager) Has to Offer Jack Smith

Guide: Bring this structure a gift. What do you bring?

Image: An amaryllis bulb. It is a bright red flower. It is not potted. It is just the bulb with a ribbon. You can watch it grow.

Interpretation: What you have to offer Jack Smith will help the business flower. It doesn't have to be packaged. Just the simple offering will be enough. And you will be able to sit back and watch your own business grow too.

Result: These insights helped Bill relax about the packaging of his sales presentation. As the imaging predicted, he found Jack Smith to be a very down-to-earth guy who welcomed what Bill could do for his company. Bill applied these insights, made a successful call, and got the account of the EVZ Company.

CONCLUSION

These are just eight examples. We could provide many more of intuitive imagery serving the needs of business people—spotting obstacles, predicting market growth or downturns in both timing and degree, and helping to resolve cultural misunderstandings with foreign customers of multinational corporations. Intuitive imaging can speed new product development, aid in strategic planning, facilitate decision making when not all the facts are in, improve relationships, help sort out personnel issues, prioritize tasks, provide a cost-effective alternative to expensive market research, and look into the future in a hundred different ways. Regardless of the size, nature, or location of your business, intuitive imagery can help it grow and prosper.

13

Conclusion

Maybe reality isn't what we see with our eyes . . .

neurosurgeon Karl Pribram

We are living at a time of info glut, nanosecond time frames, and accelerating rates of change—a time when many of the systems on which our society rests are being pushed to their limits. Such pressures are making it obvious to more and more people that we need new ways of thinking and being if we are to survive and pass on a viable society to our descendants.

A host of new trends that we mentioned in chapter 2 indicate that people are exploring these new ways of being and thinking now. We see new forms of interacting and relating among people and new paradigms appearing in all the institutions of our culture. One of these, the new paradigm in science, is described at length in chapter 3.

We also are seeing the emergence of new ways of doing business and new business models that operate with powerful new tools and techniques—like intuition and imagery, discussed in chapter 4—that enable progressive business people to grapple with the challenges of a world in transition. These tools and techniques are effective because they are nonlinear, holistic, rapid, and reliable.

The tools and techniques also rely on whole-brain approaches—approaches that allow the most successful business men and women to use more of their brain power than ever before. These leaders of business recognize that working smarter is the only way to survive in the new business climate.

Intuitive imagery is one of the most powerful of these new technologies. It is also one of the simplest, with just six easy steps, which are spelled out in chapters 5 through 10. When you use intuitive imagery, you put yourself in touch with all the knowledge, information, insight, and wisdom you need to thrive in our evolving world.

As emphasized throughout this book and demonstrated in chapters 11 and 12, through examples from the lives of ordinary people, the wisdom of the world is within you. You don't have to be a rocket scientist, a guru, or dependent on an army of experts. You really are in possession of the knowledge you need. You really can make key decisions. You really do have the answers to your questions. You only need a way to get at your inner wisdom, past the gatekeeper of the analytical left brain.

For thousands of people, intuitive imagery has been that way into their inner wisdom. We hope that having read this book, you will recognize the potential intuitive imagery offers to enrich your life and your business, to bring you fulfillment, and to help you make a real difference in the world.

The best hope for our businesses, for our personal lives, and for our planet lies in changing how we know what we know. This will redefine our place in the world. We will begin to see ourselves as connected and interdependent instead of separate and alone. Then we will begin to change how and why we do what we do. This will change the world.

Where Are You?

The three chapters of Part I provide the social context and scientific background for the process of intuitive imaging. We describe those discoveries in the natural and social sciences and the paradigmatic changes going on in our culture that are behind the growing use of imagery. Some of these discoveries and changes may be familiar to you; others may not, depending on your experience, interests, and personality type or social style.

We created the following questionnaire to help you determine where you might begin reading this book. For each statement place the numerical value corresponding to your choice in the column to the right (see the rating scale). When you finish, follow the instructions at the end of the questionnaire to score and interpret your results. (Note: There are no "right" or "wrong" answers.)

Rating Scale: Give the statements below values according to the following scale:

5 = always or very much
4 = frequently or most of the time
3 = occasionally or somewhat
2 = rarely or a little bit
1 = never or not at all

Statement	Value
I often have hunches or premonitions about people or situations.	
I act upon the hunches I have.	
When I'm driving my car in dense fog I can usually identify an object ahead of me more quickly than most people.	
When I hear of a new discovery or insight I can very easily think of ways to apply it.	
I like to focus on the "big picture" more than on details.	
I tend to get into action and learn by doing.	
I am future oriented and like to consider new possibilities.	
Other people consider me to be dynamic and somewhat undisciplined in my approach.	
I am impatient with details and analysis.	
I'm not impressed by facts. It's more important that the process work for me.	

I enjoy the following:
  Drawing and artwork, dancing and movement
  Big ideas and possibilities
  Social gatherings; expressing myself
  Daydreaming and creative reverie
  Being in action; *doing* things	

I tend *not* to enjoy the following:
  Working with facts and figures
  Setting priorities
  Being reserved and thoughtful
  Implementing a plan
  Focusing on the past	

I usually record (write or tape) the dreams I have.	
I rely on my dreams for input or guidance in living my life.	

Statement	Value
I practice meditation regularly.	
I incorporate insights I get during meditation into my life.	
When I am listening to a speech I prefer to have a casual organization rather than a step-by-step development of the points with a tight organization.	
My close friends tend to be creative or imaginative rather than practical or down-to-earth.	
I prefer to take risks rather than to be cautious.	
I prefer to speculate or theorize rather than to get involved in the nitty gritty.	
I prefer to think about problems rather than jump in and solve them "hands on."	
I think it is better to be creative than to be pragmatic.	
I stress planning for the future.	
I am more interested in what is possible than in what is actual.	
When I am reading a book I prefer a style full of analogies and metaphors rather than a straightforward or factual presentation.	
When I do ordinary things I am more likely to do them my way rather than the usual way.	
I find visionaries fascinating.	
I am more interested in design and research than in manufacturing and distribution.	
I consider myself more ingenious than practical.	
I feel it is more important for a person to have a vivid imagination rather than a strong sense of reality.	
Visions of the future are more important to me than the wisdom of the past.	

Statement	*Value*
I read novels (fiction) on a regular basis (i.e., several novels a year).	
My friends praise me for my imagination.	
I think of myself as operating more in the future than in the present.	
I prefer to start things up and then leave the running of the operation to others.	
If I am hiring an employee I stress more his or her vision than his or her experience.	
I find the subject of intuitive imagery appealing.	
I have participated in guided visualization or other visioning processes.	
When I'm working on a problem or issue, I find that answers come to me in flashes of insight or through dreams, sometimes unexpectedly.	
Sometimes I know things without knowing how I know.	
I believe in the efficacy of alternative healing practices that work with the body's natural energy system or with inner images to promote or accelerate healing.	
I believe in the power of mind to affect the physical world.	
I believe that what we experience as "reality" arises out of our thoughts, images, and beliefs.	
I believe that we are all interconnected at the level of mind.	
I am able to sense or "read" the energy in a place or from a person or group.	
I can sense when someone is staring at me from across a room.	
I am familiar with the concepts of the collective unconscious, morphogenetic fields, or archetypal images.	

Statement	Value
I am a risker. I like to just jump in and experience things. That's how I learn best.	
I am drawn to Eastern philosophies that emphasize the importance of inner realities.	
I believe that creating a vision of the desired future is an important step in achieving it.	
Total score:	

Scoring and Interpretation

Where should you begin with this book? Add your totals in the Value column. If you scored between 200 and 250, you are likely to find Part I familiar; you would be comfortable jumping right into Part II of the book and reading Part I later as confirming information. If you scored between 150 and 200, you incorporate many elements of intuitive imagery into your life already; consider beginning with Part II. If you scored between 100 and 150, you are likely to find Part I useful, informative, and necessary for you to feel comfortable with the imaging process. If you scored between 0 and 100, hold on to your socks as you read all parts of this book. It may challenge your current worldview!

Relaxation Exercises and Affirmations

In chapter 6 we spoke of relaxation as the second step of the intuitive imaging formula. Many exercises can help you relax. In this appendix we offer several types: stress reduction, mental focusing, breathing, and use of the imagination. Try them all and pick what works best for you. The final section of this appendix contains sample affirmations and space for you to create your own.

CLEARING YOUR BODY OF STRESS

Head and Neck Exercise   This simple exercise is helpful in releasing tension in the neck and aiding the natural flow of energy through the cerebrospinal system. It should be done very slowly and gently.

- Allow your head to fall gently forward three times, backward three times, to the right side three times, and then to the left side three times.
- Let the head fall gently forward. Very slowly rotate the head around to the right until your complete three full circles. Repeat this with three head rotations to the left.

Progressive Muscle Tension and Relaxation   Tensing the body's muscles floods them with revitalizing energy, clears them of stress, and helps the body to relax. Try this simple exercise. Different muscles are tensed and held in a progression from the feet to the head until the entire body is in a state of tension and then relaxed as follows. It is helpful to close your eyes. You can do this exercise sitting, standing, or lying down.

- Gently tense and hold the muscles in this progression: left foot, right foot; left calf, right calf; left upper leg, right upper leg; left buttock, right buttock; the abdominal muscles; left forearm, right forearm; left upper arm, right upper arm; chest muscles; neck muscles; and finally the muscles in the face and head.
- Take a deep breath and hold the tension in the body for a count of six, visualizing energy flowing into your muscles.
- Exhale slowly with an audible *hahhh* sound, simultaneously relaxing the muscles from head to feet. Feel the gentle outflow of energy as you relax your body and let go of tension.
- Do this exercise three to six times.

FOCUSING THE MIND

The Power of Music and Sound   Music has the power to affect the body and mind through both the rhythm and the tonal qualities. The beat and rhythm of music affect the heartbeat and respiration rate. Different tones are felt in different areas of the body through the principle of resonance. The knowledge of this is ancient. Slow, relaxing, soothing, nonlyrical instrumental music or the sound of slow, repetitive drumming is generally most appropriate for centering the mind and opening the higher intuitive centers in the body. In addition, natural sounds such as the ocean, the running water of a gentle stream, the sound of raindrops, the resonating sound of a bell, whale song, or birds singing are all excellent sounds to allow the mind to relax and become more receptive. Some new age music integrates natural sounds. Most music stores can help you choose appropriate music.

Exercise Here's how to begin to choose the ideal music to help you become centered. Select an appropriate piece of music. Sit in a comfortable position. Close your eyes and let your eyeballs roll gently upward and inward. Let yourself be carried along by the music.

Notice your breathing and respiration rate. Did the music allow you to become even more relaxed than when you started? Why or why not?

_____

_____

_____

_____

Where in your body did you *feel* the music? How did that help or hinder your focus?

_____

_____

_____

_____

Experiment with different selections of music or sounds. Which is most effective?

_____

_____

_____

_____

How can you mentally bring these sounds with you to help you relax in a noisy or stressful setting? Can you close your eyes and hear your favorite relaxing piece of music? Can you close your eyes and hear the sound of the ocean or birds singing on a fresh spring morning?

_____

_____

_____

_____

Focusing with a Phrase   Some Eastern meditative practices teach each individual devotee a personal mantra. The mantra is a Sanskrit word with a special meaning. Both the meaning and the sound are important in helping to focus the mind. An example is repeating the Sanskrit word *Aum,* which is said to carry the vibrations of the universal life force. In the United States, research on the relaxation response has shown that even repeating the word *one* over and over again in the mind has a calming effect and produces more alpha brain waves. This may be because *one* stands for unity, which is integrative. In any event, choosing a word or phrase that has a special calming effect or special personal meaning can help focus the mind. A phrase that acted as a verbal focusing tool for me when I was in my twenties came from my experience in Edgar Cayce study groups. It was "Be still and know that I am God." It came to have a special meaning for me. Choose a phrase that has special meaning for you.

Exercise

What word or phrase has a special meaning for you that is calming, that helps still your mind?

_____

_____

_____

_____

Close your eyes and relax. Repeat your focusing phrase several times out loud. Then repeat this phrase to yourself, allowing its meaning to sink into your mind. Notice your reactions. How did you feel after saying the focusing phrase?

_____

_____

_____

_____

Using a Higher Quality as a Focusing Word   It is also effective to choose a specific higher quality that you want to strengthen in your life. These can include joy, love, truth, happiness, freedom, aliveness, courage, fulfillment, growth, prosperity, or bliss. Choose a quality that you would like more present in your life. Sit comfortably, close your eyes, and relax. Repeat the word aloud softly several times. The sound is important. Allow it to resonate through you as you say it. Then repeat the word mentally as you bring its meaning into your mind and its feeling into your body. Become fully associated with it.

How did you feel after using this higher quality as a focusing word? Record your experience.

_____

_____

_____

_____

In what situations can you use a focusing word or phrase to help you become more centered?

_____

_____

_____

_____

The Power of Vision   The eyes are connected directly to the brain. Roughly seventy percent of all the input we receive consciously and subconsciously about our reality comes to us through sight. This fact makes vision the most powerful sense we have. We can use this power to still the constant activity of our minds by focusing our vision on an object, shape, or picture. The object becomes a visual mantra to occupy the mind, stop the flow of inner images, and quiet our logical self-talk. Choose an object or geometric shape on which to focus. Almost anything will work, but selecting something with a spiritual significance to you will increase the power of this visual mantra (see the archetypal symbols in chapter 9). In focusing, the key is to *gaze* at an object with *soft eyes*. Instead of staring intently, it is desirable to relax the vision and let the eyes go ever so slightly out of focus.

Candle Meditation   You can use this same meditation with similar results with other objects, pictures, or mandalas (images with a spiritual significance). I've chosen a candle because the flame always signified the light of the Spirit to me. (This meditation is adapted from Millman 1992.)

- Select a candle with a good-sized flame.
- Set it down away from flammable objects. Position it so that the flame is about twelve to eighteen inches in front of you.
- Take a deep breath, relax, and center yourself. Imagine yourself surrounded by the loving light of the Spirit.
- Gaze into the flame. Keep blinking to a minimum. Fill your mind with the image of the flame.
- Imagine that the candle acts like a vacuum cleaner. As thoughts or images drift into your awareness, imagine them being pulled into the flame and disappearing into the ethers.
- Do this meditation for three to five minutes.

What did you experience in this meditation? Did your mind become centered? Were you able to let go of your self-talk and mental chatter?

_____

_____

_____

_____

What other objects, pictures, or mandalas would work for you in this focusing exercise?

_____

_____

_____

_____

Focusing the Senses   For each of us to take full advantage of our intuitions and inner images, it is important for our senses to remain clear and focused in the present moment. This next exercise has the potential to heighten our senses and bring them together in an integrated whole. When this happens, all your sensations become a "single highly focused brilliant point of perception" (Ashley 1984). Every sense becomes more highly attuned. Sounds become clearer. Colors become more intense. Objects take on a new dimension of depth. Your awareness becomes unified and connected with everything around you. It is a truly marvelous experience.

Here and Now   Do this exercise (from Ashley 1984) for five or ten minutes a day. Commit to doing it every day for an entire week, if possible. Find a quiet place outdoors in a natural setting where there are some trees.

Sitting Exercise   Sit quietly. Relax and center yourself. Slowly look around you. Become aware of your surroundings. Ask yourself, "What am I conscious of right now?" Take in everything:

- Sight: the colors, shapes, and textures
- Sound: birds singing, distant cars, people talking, the breeze in the leaves

- Touch: the feel of the wind on your face, the temperature, the pressure of your body against the ground
- Smell: the fragrance of the flowers, the smells of nature
- Taste: what you are tasting in your mouth right now

As vividly as possible, experience the scene with all your senses. Then close your eyes. Experience the same scene. Concentrate on the inner experience this time. How is it different? Become aware of the many sounds that you may not have noticed before. Identify them, mentally connecting the sound with the object that makes it. Feel your body as part of the natural surroundings. Are your hands cold or hot? What other sensations do you feel in your body? Do you have a taste in your mouth? Of what smells are you conscious? Stretch your awareness. Sense your connection with nature.

Open your eyes and bring the inner and the outer together. Feel your connection through the senses with nature. Become aware of the interconnectedness of all natural phenomena. Feel yourself a part of this process of nature. *Feel* this interaction. Feel all your sensations come together and form a unified whole. Feel your hearing and your vision, your tasting and your smelling, your touch, feel them as *one* brilliant perception. Hold this perception in your mind, then close your eyes again.

Let this sense of unity fade and sounds become dominant. Follow one particular sound closely, concentrating on it, following it in your mind. Then open your eyes and instantly once again bring your sense together into a unified whole, all your sensations adding up to a single highly focused brilliant point of perception.

After you have done this a few times and are aware of the contrast between perceiving one thing at a time and perceiving a unified whole, you will develop a *feeling* for this unity. You will recognize how you feel when your consciousness is totally in the here and now, focused totally in physical reality. Over time, as you experience this unity of mind and body, you will find that you are able to concentrate better and receive richer, clearer images.

Every day that you do this focusing exercise, record your experience: Were you able to integrate all of your senses? What happened to your sense of sight, sound, smell, taste, and touch? Did you have the sense of being totally present in the here and now? Did you experience your connection with nature? What happened to your perception of the world around you?

Day 1: _____

_____

_____

_____

Day 2: _____

_____

_____

_____

Day 3: _____

_____

_____

_____

Day 4: _____

_____

_____

_____

Day 5: _____

_____

_____

_____

Day 6: _____

_____

_____

_____

Day 7: _____

_____

_____

_____

Walking Integration   This is a variation on the previous exercise that I developed. I used to do it as I was walking my dog in the early mornings. It can be just as powerful as the sitting exercise.

Take a slow walk for fifteen to twenty minutes, preferably by yourself. Play with being in nature in a way that brings all your senses together in a unified perception. Some of you may experience a *home station* as all your senses integrate, much like tuning in a radio station to its clearest point. Be aware if this happens and where in the body you experience it.

Notice any changes in the normal experience of your sensory input, such as colors changing in hue or intensity, peripheral vision expanding, sounds or smells becoming more acute, and so on.

When you get to the point that all your senses become unified into one brilliant perception, stretch out with your feelings to experience each thing you see. Without physically touching what you encounter, extend your awareness to become one with it. *Become* the trees, the leaves blowing in the breeze, the flowers, the earth, the rocks, and the moss. *Feel* them with your mind. *Feel* the birds, animals, butterflies, and people you meet.

How much was your rational *observer* active in judging what you were experiencing? How did that help or hinder you?

_____

_____

_____

_____

What was your experience of being totally present in the
here and now?

_____

_____

_____

_____

What was different from normal consciousness?

_____

_____

_____

_____

How can you recognize this place? Did you get a sense of
finding a *home station?* Where in your body did you feel it?

_____

_____

_____

_____

How did you experience your connection with nature?
Did you get to a place of unity?

_____

_____

_____

_____

BREATHING

Breathe in the manner that is normal for you.

Do you breathe into your chest or your belly? Chest breathing activates the right brain (analytical); diaphragmatic or "belly" breathing activates the left brain (intuitive). Which hemisphere of the brain are you activating?

_____

_____

_____

_____

The Cleansing Breath   This is a simple breathing technique to release negative energy and feelings that may impede or obstruct us in receiving clear images. When we inhale, we can breathe in more than just oxygen. We can also breathe in life energy, light, love, and happiness. When we exhale, we can breathe out not only carbon dioxide but also mental and emotional toxins, like frustrations, fears, worries, sorrow, and anger. The following exercise (from Millman, 1992) is very useful for self-cleansing:

- As you inhale, visualize and feel that you are taking in light, healing energy and love.
- As you exhale slowly and fully, visualize and feel yourself breathing out any negative energy or feelings. Breathe out any "darker" energy. Breathe out any fear, worry, sadness, or anger.
- Continue breathing in this manner for one or two minutes.

Use the cleansing breath to release negative emotions. Compare your feelings before and after. Were you able to breathe out the darker energy? Does your body feel different?

_____

_____

_____

_____

How can you use the cleansing breath in your life to release unwanted emotions?

_____

_____

_____

_____

Shifting Brain States   Here are four very simple breathing exercises that will lower brain wave activity and increase your intuitive and imaging abilities. The first is a very simple yogic breathing exercise.

- Close your eyes.
- Inhale in long, slow comfortable breaths.
- Breathe deeply, feeling your inhalation expand your belly and lower back, then your chest.
- As you inhale, feel your body filled with vitality.
- As you exhale, feel your shoulders, chest, belly, and entire body relax and let go of tension.
- Make each exhalation about the same length as the inhalation.
- Allow each outgoing breath to be more relaxed than the one before it.
- Continue breathing in this manner for two to five minutes.

This next breathing protocol was developed by Win Wenger, one of the nation's foremost experts on genius and intelligence. This exercise can be used to decrease mental noise and improve mental functioning (see Kenyon 1994):

- Sit comfortably and close your eyes.
- Imagine and feel that your body is a hollow tube and that as you inhale, the breath is drawn up through your feet and into your legs; up into your pelvis and stomach; up into

your chest and back; and up into your shoulders, neck, and head.

- Imagine and feel your breath swishing through the hollow tube of your body and carrying away any tension, stress, or uncomfortable feelings.
- When you get to the top of the inhalation, just relax and exhale normally. Let each exhalation be more relaxed than the one before it.
- Let your breathing be long, slow, and comfortable. Breathe in this way for a minimum of two to five minutes.

The following simple breathing exercise was developed by Edgar Cayce as a preparation to enter meditation. It acts to produce an integrated, more receptive brain state:

- Sit comfortably and close your eyes.
- Breathe in slowly through the right nostril and exhale slowly through the mouth. Do this three times.
- Breathe in slowly through the left nostril and exhale slowly through the right nostril. Do this three times.
- Repeat this twice more for a total of three complete cycles.
- Make sure to take in full, deep breaths that expand the belly and the chest.
- The entire process takes about three minutes. Don't rush it.

The next exercise is another yogic breathing pattern that has the ability to profoundly alter awareness, lower brain wave activity, and enhance intuition:

- Sit comfortably.
- Close your eyes. Allow your eyeballs to rotate gently upward and inward.
- Adjust your posture so that your spine is straight, and your head is level with the floor.

- Inhale slowly to a count of seven. (Let each count equal about one second. Count one thousand one, one thousand two, one thousand three, and so on.)
- Hold the in breath to a count of seven.
- Exhale to a count of seven.
- Pause for a count of three before inhaling again.
- Repeat this sequence six more times for a total of seven.
- After you have mastered breathing to a seven count, increase your breathing to a count of eleven, and repeat the sequence a total of eleven times.

Choose one of the four exercises and breathe in the instructed manner for two to five minutes. Open your eyes and write down any observations or impressions you have.

_____

_____

_____

_____

Experience how your body feels. Do you notice any differences? How do you feel inside your head? Do you feel lighter or floaty?

_____

_____

_____

_____

How does your body feel? Did you feel a tingling sensation in any part of your body?

_____

_____

_____

_____

Do you feel more alert? More energized? More relaxed?

_____

_____

_____

_____

Look around you. Observe your perception of objects. Are they sharper or more in focus? Do colors look different to you?

_____

_____

_____

_____

Notice your sense of hearing. Is anything different? Do sounds seem clearer?

_____

_____

_____

_____

USING YOUR IMAGINATION TO RELAX

I like to use this guided visualization to help people identify their dominant imaging sense: sight, hearing, touch, taste, or smell. It is adapted from William Fezler's excellent book, *Creative Imagery: How to Visualize in All Five Senses.*

Garden Scene Close your eyes and relax. Imagine that you are in the middle of a vast garden, a garden that stretches for miles and miles. It is midnight. It is midsummer. The moon is full and *silver*, the sky is clear, filled with stars. The air is *warm* and balmy. Begin to see leaves of brilliant *green*, shimmering in the moonlight. And hear the *low, soft* rustle of a breeze through the leaves.

You are walking down a path on either side of which are tall lemon trees laden with lemons. They glow phosphorescent in the moonlight, a brilliant yellow against deep *green* foliage. The lemons are ripe. They hang heavy from their branches. There are lemons on the ground. The sweet scent of lemons permeates the air.

Reach up. Pick a lemon. Feel the coarse outer surface of the peel. Peel the fruit. Feel the soft, moist inner surface. Bite into the lemon. The *sour lemon* juice squirts into your mouth and you feel your mouth pucker from its tartness.

Continue walking and come to a long, descending *white* marble staircase, glistening in the moonlight. Begin to descend the stairs. With each step downward, you go deeper and deeper and become more and more relaxed. When you reach the base of the stairs you are in a profound state of relaxation. The night sky is above you. The velvety soft moonlight bathes you in beauty. And you drift, you float, and dream. . . .

Stay with this as long as you want to. Then answer the following questions:

What did you experience?

_____

_____

_____

_____

What was your dominant imaging sense? Were you able to see, hear, taste, feel, and smell?

_____

_____

_____

_____

The next image is less structured. It allows your own images to emerge (adapted from Saunders and McKnew 1992):

Nature Scene   Imagine yourself in a peaceful place in nature. Imagine a place that is pleasant and comfortable. It may be a real place that you know, or it may be a place that exists only in your image world. As you go to this special place in your imagination, allow yourself to become free of worry, just for this special time. Take some time to look around and notice what's there. As you engage each of your senses, you experience a feeling of freedom and joy. Listen to sounds. Pay attention to whatever you can smell there. Touch something if you want to. Taste the air. Be aware of all the different things there. The earth, the air, maybe there is water, maybe rocks, trees, other vegetation, maybe birds or other animal life. Let yourself be aware of how different all of these are and yet how they are all there together. Watch how they interact with each other, how they affect each other. Stay with this as long as you want to.

Record your personal nature scene so you can go back to this place whenever you want to relax:

_____

_____

_____

_____

Your Personal Place   Take a moment to allow yourself to find the imaginary place where you feel most relaxed and receptive. It may be a real place that you know, or it may be a place that exists only in your image world. It can be on a mountain top in summer or a mountain where you are racing downhill on a pair of snow skis. It can be a tropical beach where you are listening to the surf gently washing the white sand. It can be a forest where you are listening to the birds singing. It can be outer space where you are experiencing weightlessness or the bridge of the starship *Enterprise*. Close your eyes and find your special place.

> Where did you go? Describe your special place. Know that you can return there any time.

> _____

> _____

> _____

> _____

Practice these images for a few minutes every day. After a week, you will find that you become relaxed more easily. You may experience feelings of lightness that are often associated with entering the alpha state. Each time you relax using your imagination like this, you become more open and receptive to your intuition and intuitive imaging.

AFFIRMATIONS

Here are some affirmations we have used in our workshops to help strengthen intuitive ability. Choose one that feels good to you, or write your own:

- Every day in every way my imaging ability grows more and more reliable.
- My images give me reliable, accurate information that I trust.
- My images get clearer and stronger each day.
- I receive powerful insights through the images and symbols in my mind.
- My inner genius brings me the answers I need through my images.
- My imaging ability is strengthened as I act on the insights I receive.

- I am open to receive with every breath that I breathe.
- I honor and trust myself.

Incorporating the spiritual can strengthen affirmations if you believe in God, Christ, Buddha, a Higher Power, or the Higher Self. Here are a couple of examples:

- My intuition reveals my Higher Self and is in harmony with Divine Guidance.
- The Christ in me now frees me from all limited thinking and guides my images.

Using the foregoing examples as a guide, formulate several affirmations of your own:

_____

_____

_____

_____

Choose an affirmation that you will faithfully repeat several times a day for one week. Record your observations each day in your imaging journal. At the end of the week see how repeating the affirmation and visualization have strengthened your imaging ability and intuitive insight.

Appendix **3**

Resources for Interpreting Images

Here are some useful reference books that can help in decoding and deciphering images, especially if you are a beginner. As we note in chapters 6 and 8, we urge you to put more weight on *your own* associations and meanings.

Boushahla, J. J., and V. Reidel-Geubtner. 1983. *The Dream Dictionary*. New York: Pilgrim Press.

Cirlot, J. E. 1962. *A Dictionary of Symbols*. New York: Philosophical Library. Cirlot draws from Eastern sources and Jungian dream work.

Cooper, J. C. 1978. *An Illustrated Encyclopedia of Traditional Symbols*. London: Thames and Hudson.

Gaskell, G. S. 1988. *Dictionary of Scripture and Myth*. New York: Dorset Press. Good for archetypal (power) symbols and images.

Hay, Louise L. 1984. *You Can Heal Your Life*. Santa Monica: Hay House. This is an excellent resource for interpreting body symbolism.

Intuitive Imaging Steps

A. Steps for doing intuitive imagery with a partner

Ask permission from your partner to access his or her intuition

Define the question you want answered; be sure to keep this question to yourself

Select a suitable guide prompt

Start the imagery process by giving your partner the guide prompt

Record the images as your partner speaks; if you are working with more than one partner, have each one write down his or her imagery

Interpret the imagery, using your *partner's* meanings and interpretations as well as your own

Record the imagery in a dated journal entry

B. Steps for doing intuitive imagery alone

Define your questions

Write your questions on index cards, a separate card for each question

193

Choose an imaging guide prompt

Bunch together questions that will work with the same prompt

Turn the index cards face down; keep them face down until the entire imagery process is over

Write the guide prompt on each card

Shuffle all the cards

Number all the cards

Pick up the first card and receive images about it

Record your images and feelings, on the card or a pad, including the number of the card; do this for each card

Turn the cards over and interpret the images in reference to your original inquiry

Date and record your results in a journal, leaving space to record at a later date what the outcome was

Tips for Doing Intuitive Imagery

A. Define the question

Only quality questions will produce quality answers

Make your questions clear and specific

Use only single questions (not compound ones that use "and" or "or")

Ask only meaningful, important questions, no trivial ones

Make sure you really want an answer to the question

B. Choose a guide question or prompt

Consult Table 7.1 for the most appropriate guide questions to ask your partner or write on your index card

If you have several different types of questions, bunch them into groups that will work with the same prompt

C. Relax and center yourself

If necessary, use a relaxation technique such as breathing or muscle tension release (see appendix 2)

Commit adequate time to the process (at least 30 minutes)

Affirm that you are open to your intuition and are ready to receive its guidance

D. Receive images

Suspend your judgment; allow whatever comes to be OK

Trust yourself

Be open to new information

Expect the unexpected

Remember that images can come in visual, auditory, or kinesthetic forms

Your first image or intuitive response is often the clearest

E. Interpret your images

Be open to accepting what an image is saying, even if it threatens current beliefs or attitudes

Recognize that imagery can be disturbingly frank, telling you things you may not want to hear

No matter how unappealing an image may seem, it holds valuable information from your higher self

Allow yourself to be puzzled

Let go of trying to understand difficult images; let them simmer in your mind; a flash of insight later on may give you clues about the meaning

Consult reference books on symbols and imagery, but recognize that the best interpreter of your images is *you*

Practice—interpreting imagery is like learning a new language, the language of your right brain

F. Keep an imagery journal

Record your imagery in dated entries

Verify the reliability of your imagery by applying its guidance and recording the results over time

Guidelines for Interpreting Images

A. Pose questions

About the image: size, brightness

From your senses: sounds, smells, colors

Relate the image to yourself: feelings in your body, the reactions you have to the image, the parts you are playing

Evaluate: What things are appealing? Displeasing? Are there puns and humor? Idiomatic phrases?

Dialogue with the image: What does it want from you? Become the image and see what message it has for you

B. Techniques

Take multiple images either individually or as a group to see their basic theme.

Rate the image on a scale of 1 to 10 (10 best), for questions in which you are evaluating a series of options, alternatives, or priorities to see which is best.

Do word association.

Do word amplification.

Incubate the image.

Consult books and experts.

Guess.

Let go and let it simmer in your mind.

Use imaging to gain more information.

C. Dealing with yes or no questions

Do imagery and evaluate the results

Positive images often are light, beautiful, friendly, close, in focus, appealing, orderly, harmonious, set in nature

Negative images often are heavy, ugly, hostile, far away, indistinct or fuzzy, unappealing, messy, dissonant, set in human-made or artificial locations

Take a shortcut: put *yes* and *no* on separate pieces of paper; shuffle them and use one of the following techniques while holding your question in mind:

Imagine one of the pieces coming toward you

Get a message telling you which is correct

Hold both; the correct one feels lighter

See the correct one light up

See a rose bud bloom on the correct one

Scan the energy; the correct one feels more energetic

D. Validate your interpretation

Test of feeling: a right interpretation feels light

Visualize *yes* or *no*

Test from content: truth is caring

Test from common sense: what would be the real-life consequences of acting on this meaning?

Resources for Further Study and Information

For further information on

- Seminars, workshops, and retreats on intuitive imagery, applied intuition, and community building
- Business consulting services
- Coaching and counseling services
- Workbooks and audio and video tapes
- Books on community building

Please contact
Creative Change Technologies
5 Sombra del Monte
Placitas, NM 87043
phone/fax: (505) 867-3068
email: jbpehrson@aol.com

Bibliography

ABC Evening News. 1996. "American Agenda: Alternative Healing Systems Used by Dr. Mehmet Oz." January 11.

Adler, Gerhard. 1961. *The Living Symbol: A Case Study in the Process of Individuation*. New York: Pantheon Books.

Agor, Weston. 1986. *The Logic of Intuitive Decision-Making*. New York: Quorum Books.

Ahsen, Akhter. 1993. "Imagery treatment of alcoholism and drug abuse: A new methodology for treatment and research." *Journal of Mental Imagery* 17:1–60.

Antonietti, Alessandro. 1991. "Why does mental visualization facilitate problem-solving." In *Mental Images in Human Cognition: Advances in Psychology*, edited by Robert Logie and Michel Denis. Amsterdam: North Holland.

Appleyard, Brian. 1992. *Understanding the Present: Science and the Soul of Modern Man*. New York: Doubleday.

Ashley, Nancy. 1984. *Create Your Own Reality*. New York: Prentice Hall.

Asimov, Isaac. 1982. *Asimov's Biographical Encyclopedia of Science and Technology*. Garden City: Doubleday.

Augros, Robert, and George Stanciu. 1984. *The New Story of Science*. New York: Bantam Books.

Autry, James. 1991. *Love and Profit: The Art of Caring Leadership*. New York: William Morrow.

Bachmann, Talis, and Monika Oit. 1992. "Stroop-like interference in chess players' imagery: An unexplored possibility to be revealed by the adapted moving-spot task." *Psychological Research* 54:27–31.

Backman, Lars, et al. 1991. "The generalizability of training gains in dementia: Effects of an imagery-based mnemonic on face-name retention duration." *Psychology and Aging* 6:489–92.

Bergland, Richard. 1985. *The Fabric of Mind.* New York: Viking Press.

Betts, L. 1995. "Imagine . . . your way to better golf." *Golf Magazine* 37 (January):48–9.

Blakeslee, Sandra. 1995. "Searching for simple rules of complexity." *New York Times* December 26.

Bly, Robert, James Hilman and Michael Meade. 1993. *Rag and Boneshop of the Heart.* New York: HarperPerennial.

Boushahla, J. J., and V. Reidel-Geubtner. 1983. *The Dream Dictionary.* New York: Pilgrim Press.

Brennan, Barbara. 1987. *Hands of Light: A Guide to Healing Through the Human Energy Field.* New York: Bantam Books.

———. 1993. *Light Emerging: The Journey of Personal Healing.* New York: Bantam Books.

Brewer, Britton, and Robert Shillinglaw. 1992. "Evaluation of a psychological skills training workshop for male intercollegiate lacrosse players." *Sport Psychologist* 6:139–47.

Butler, Richard. 1993. "Establishing a dry run: A case study in securing bladder control." *British Journal of Clinical Psychology* 32:215–7.

Campbell, Joseph. 1949. *The Hero with a Thousand Faces.* New York: Pantheon Books.

———. 1976. *The Masks of God: Primitive Mythology.* New York: Penguin Books.

Chemical Bank. 1992. "With intellectual currency capital strength is more than just money in the bank." *New York Times* March 19.

Cirlot, J. E. 1962. *A Dictionary of Symbols.* New York: Philosophical Library.

Cooper, J. C. 1978. *An Illustrated Encyclopedia of Traditional Symbols.* London: Thames and Hudson.

Commoner, Barry. 1971. *The Closing Circle: Nature, Man and Technology.* New York: Alfred A. Knopf.

Creen, Ted. 1992. "Through the valley of the shadow: Developing a visualization process for healing grief." In *Spiritual, Ethical and Pastoral Aspects of Death and Bereavement,* edited by Gerry Cox and Ronald Fundis. Death, Value and Meaning Series. Amityville: Baywood Publishing Company.

Davies, Paul. 1993. "The holy grail of physics." *New York Times* March 7.

Deschaumes-Molinari, C., et al. 1991. "Relationship between mental imagery and sporting performance." *Behavioural Brain Research* 45:29–36.

Didron, Alphonse N. 1965. *Christian Iconography: The History of Christian Art in the Middle Ages.* 2 vols. New York: Frederick Ungar Publishing Co.

Dossey, Larry. 1993. *Healing Words: The Power of Prayer and the Practice of Medicine.* New York: HarperCollins.

Downing, Frances. 1992. "Image banks: Dialogues between the past and the future." *Environment and Behavior* 24:441–70.

Egan, Timothy. 1996. "Seattle officials seeking to establish a subsidized natural medicine clinic." *New York Times* January 3.

Eisler, Riane. 1987. *The Chalice and the Blade: Our History, Our Future.* San Francisco: Harper and Row.

Ekins, Paul, ed. 1986. *The Living Economy.* London: Routledge and Kegan Paul.

Eliade, Mircea. 1960. *Myths, Dreams and Mysteries: The Encounter Between Contemporary Faiths and Archaic Realities.* New York: Harper.

Emery, Marcia. 1994. *Dr. Marcia Emery's Intuition Workbook: An Expert's Guide to Unlocking the Wisdom of Your Subconscious Mind.* Englewood Cliffs: Prentice Hall.

———. 1995. "Power Hunches." *Hemispheres* (December):41–4.

Epstein, Gerald. 1989. *Healing Visualizations: Creating Health Through Imagery.* New York: Bantam Books.

Fanning, Patrick. 1988. *Visualization for Change.* Oakland: New Harbinger Publications.

Feigl, Herbert. 1973. "Positivism in the Twentieth Century." *Dictionary of the History of Ideas,* vol. III, 545–51. New York: Charles Scribner's Sons.

Ferguson, Marilyn. 1980. *The Aquarian Conspiracy.* Los Angeles: J.P. Tarcher.

Fezler, William. 1989. *Creative Imagery: How to Visualize in All Five Senses.* New York: Simon and Schuster.

Freeman, Arthur, and Suzanne Boyd. 1992. "The use of dreams and the dream metaphor in cognitive-behavior therapy." *Psychotherapy in Private Practice* 10:173–92.

Friedman, Norman. 1994. *Bridging Science and Spirit: Common Elements in David Bohm's Physics, The Perennial Philosophy and Seth.* St. Louis: Living Lake Books.

Gage, G. Robert. 1993. "And protect the data." *New York Times* March 14.

Gaskell, G. S. 1988. *Dictionary of Scripture and Myth.* New York: Dorsett Press.

Gazzaniga, Michael. 1976. "The Biology of Memory." *Neural Mechanisms of Learning and Memory,* edited by M. Rosenzweig and E. Bennett. Cambridge: MIT Press.

———, and Joseph LeDoux. 1978. *The Integrated Mind.* New York: Plenum Press.

Good Morning America. 1996. "Visualizing is the key." *The New York Daily News* January 16.

Greenspan, Alan. 1992. "International Financial Integration." Speech given to Federation of Bankers Associations of Japan, Tokyo, October 14.

Grouios, George. 1992. "The effect of mental practice on diving performance." *International Journal of Sports Psychology* 23:60–9.

Hansell, Saul. 1993. "The man who charged up Mastercard." *New York Times* March 7.

Harman, Willis. 1988. *Global Mind Change.* Indianapolis: Knowledge Systems.

———. 1993. "Two liberating concepts for research on consciousness." *Noetic Sciences Review Spring,* 14–6.

Harman, Willis, and Howard Rheingold. 1984. *Higher Creativity: Liberating the Unconscious for Breakthrough Insights.* Sausalito: Institute of Noetic Sciences.

Hay, Louise. 1984. *You Can Heal Your Life.* Santa Monica: Hay House.

Hilgard, Ernest. 1981. "Imagery and imagination in American psychology." *Journal of Mental Imagery* V:5–66.

Hilts, Philip. 1993. "FDA ends ban on women in drug testing." *New York Times* March 25.

——— 1995. "Health maintenance organizations turn to spiritual healing." *New York Times* December 17.

Hochschild, Adam. 1993. "A cartel is forever." *New York Times* August 8.

Hopcke, Robert. 1989. *A Guided Tour of the Collected Works of C. G. Jung.* Boston: Shambhala Publications.

Howe, Maurice. 1989. "Using imagery to facilitate organizational development and change." *Group and Organization Studies* (March):70.

Jacobi, Jolande. 1959. *Complex/Archetype/Symbol in the Psychology of C. G. Jung.* Princeton: Princeton University Press.

Jacobs, Michael. 1991. "A failure of nerve on banking reform." *New York Times* December 8.

Jahn, Robert, and Brenda Dunne. 1987. *Margins of Reality: The Role of Consciousness in the Physical World.* New York: Harcourt Brace Jovanovich.

Jampole, Ellen. 1991. "Effects of imagery training on the creative writing of academically gifted elementary students." *National Reading Conference Yearbook* 40:313–8.

Jennings, Jerry. 1991. "Aphorisms and the creative imagination: Lessons in creativity, method and communication." *Journal of Mental Imagery* 15:111–32.

Jung, Carl. 1959. *Collected Works,* vol. 9.2. Princeton: Princeton University Press.

———. 1971. "Individual dream symbolism in relation to alchemy." In *The Portable Jung.* New York: Penguin Books.

Jung, Carl, et al. 1961. *Man and His Symbols.* New York: Dell Publishing Co.

———. 1965. *Memories, Dreams, Reflections.* New York: Vintage Books.

———. 1953. "Psychology and Alchemy." In *Collected Works,* vol. 12. Princeton: Princeton University Press.

————. 1976. "The Symbolic Life." In *Collected Works*, vol. 18. Princeton: Princeton University Press.

Keen, Sam. 1992. "Dying Gods and Borning Spirits." *Noetic Sciences Review* Winter, 24–8.

Keirsey, David, and Marilyn Bates. 1984. *Please Understand Me: Character and Temperament Types*. Del Mar, Calif.: Prometheus Nemesis Books.

Keller, Evelyn Fox. 1983. *A Feeling for the Organism: The Life and Work of Barbara McClintock*. New York: W. H. Freeman.

Kenyon, Tom. 1994. *Brain States*. Naples, Fla.: United States Publishing.

Kerényi, C. 1976. *Dionysos: Archetypal Image of Indestructible Life*. Princeton: Princeton University Press.

Kilner, Walter. 1965. *The Human Aura*. New Hyde Park: University Books.

Koestler, Arthur. 1964. *The Act of Creation*. New York: Macmillan.

Konopak, Bonnie, et al. 1991. "Use of mnemonic imagery for content learning." *Journal of Reading, Writing and Learning Disabilities International* 7:309–19.

Korol, Christine, and Carl von Baeyer. 1992. "Effects of brief instruction in imagery and birth visualization in pre-natal education." *Journal of Mental Imagery* 16:167–72.

Kosslyn, Stephen. 1994. *Image and Brain: The Resolution of the Imagery Debate*. Cambridge: MIT Press.

Krieger, Dolores. 1979. *The Therapeutic Touch: How to Use Your Hands to Help or Heal*. Englewood Cliffs: Prentice-Hall.

Krieger, Leonard. 1973. "Authority." *Dictionary of the History of Ideas*, vol. I, 141–62. New York: Charles Scribner's Sons.

Land, George, and Beth Jarman. 1992. *Breakpoint and Beyond: Mastering the Future Today*. New York: Harper Business.

Leary, Warren. 1993. "Science takes a lesson from nature, imitating abalone and spider silk." *New York Times* August 31.

Libet, Benjamin. 1980. "Mental phenomena and behavior." *The Behavioral and Brain Sciences* 3:434.

————. 1985. "Unconscious cerebral initiative and the role of conscious will in voluntary action." *The Behavioral and Brain Sciences* 8:529–66.

————. 1987. "Awareness of wanting to move and of moving." *The Behavioral and Brain Sciences* 10:320–1.

Liggett, Donald, and Sadao Hamada. 1993. "Enhancing the visualization of gymnasts." *American Journal of Clinical Hypnosis* 35:190–7.

Lindauer, Martin. 1983. "Imagery and the arts." In *Imagery: Current Theory, Research and Application*, edited by A. Sheikh. 472–500. New York: John Wiley and Sons.

Luzzato, Paolo. 1994. "Anorexia nervosa and art therapy: The 'double trap' of the anorexic patient." *Arts in Psychotherapy* 21:139–43.

Mandel, Terry. 1993. "Giving values a voice: marketing in the new paradigm." *The New Business Paradigm,* edited by M. Ray and A. Rinzler. New York: Jeremy Tarcher/Perigee Books.

McGarvey, Robert. 1992. "Picture yourself a winner." *Reader's Digest* (July):126.

Metzner, Ralph. 1993. "The split between spirit and nature in western consciousness." *Noetic Sciences Review* (Spring): 4–9

Millman, Dan. 1992. *No Ordinary Moments: A Peaceful Warrior's Guide to Daily Life.* Tiburon, Calif.: H. J. Kramer.

Mollner, Terry. 1988. "The third way is here." In *Context,* Autumn.

Mossman, Magaly R., and James F. Mossman. 1987. *Light Imagery Work.* Self-published. Minneapolis. Rapid Change Technologies.

Munson, M. 1995. "A plug for hearing." *Prevention* 47 (May):24.

Murphy, Michael. 1992. *The Future of the Body: Explorations Into the Further Evolution of Human Nature.* New York: G. P. Putnam's Sons.

Myrick, Robert, and Linda Myrick. 1993. "Guided imagery: From mystical to practical." *Elementary School Guidance and Counseling* 28:62–70.

Nadel, Laurie, et al. 1990. *Sixth Sense: The Whole Brain Book of Intuition, Hunches, Gut Feelings, and Their Place in Your Everyday Life.* New York: Prentice Hall.

Naisbitt, John, and Patricia Aburdene. 1985. *Reinventing the Corporation.* New York: Warner Books.

———. 1990. *Megatrends 2000.* New York: Avon Books.

Naparstek, Belleruth. 1994. *Staying Well with Guided Imagery.* New York: Warner Books.

Neck, Chris, and Charles Manz. 1992. "Thought self-leadership: The influence of self-talk and mental imagery on performance." *Journal of Organizational Behavior* (December):681.

Neumeier, Mike. 1990. "You're better than you think." *Institutional Distribution* (March):34.

Norris, Floyd. 1992. "Why currencies move faster than politics." *New York Times* September 23.

Norton, Rob. 1991. "The most fascinating ideas for 1991." *Fortune* January 14.

Ostrander, Sheila, and Lynn Schroeder. 1974. *Handbook of Psychic Discoveries.* New York: Berkley Books.

Palmer, Shawna. 1992. "A comparison of mental practice techniques as applied to the developing competitive figure skater." *Sport Psychologist* 6:148–55.

Parikh, Jagdish. 1994. *Intuition: The New Frontier of Management.* Oxford: Blackwell Publishers.

Passell, Peter. 1992. "Fast money." *New York Times* October 10.

Pert, Candace. 1987. "Neuropeptides, the Emotions and Bodymind." *Consciousness and Survival*, edited by J. Spong. Sausalito: Institute of Noetic Sciences.

Pollack, Andrew. 1995. "The life force in the briefcase." *New York Times* November 28.

Popcorn, Faith. 1991. *The Popcorn Report*. New York: Doubleday Currency.

Rancour, Patrice. 1991. "Guided imagery: Healing when curing is out of the question." *Perspectives in Psychiatric Care* 27:30–3.

Ray, Michael, and Rochelle Myers. 1986. *Creativity in Business*. Garden City: Doubleday and Co.

———, and Alan Rinzler. 1993. *The New Business Paradigm*. New York: Jeremy Tarcher/Perigee Books.

Reed, Henry. 1994. *Dream Solutions, Dream Realizations: The Original Programmed Workbook Bringing You Intuitive Guidance from Dreams*, 7th ed. Virginia Beach, VA: Regal Copy.

Ricci, Claudia. 1995. "The eros of everyday life." *New York Times Book Review* December 31.

Richardson, Alan. 1983. "Imagery: definition and types." In *Imagery: Current Theory, Research and Application*, edited by A. Sheikh, pp. 13–36. New York: John Wiley and Sons.

Roman, Sanaya, and Duane Packer. 1988. *Creating Money*. Tiburon, Calif.: H. J. Kramer.

Rowland, Mary. 1992. "A farewell to paternalism." *New York Times* March 8.

Saul, John Ralston. 1992. "Paper games and monetary chaos." *New York Times* October 9.

Saunders, Marilyn, and Gretchen McKnew. 1992. *Using Imagery in Therapy: A Path to Nurturance, Empowerment and Reconciliation*. Bethesda: Imagery Training Institute.

Savoy, Carolyn. 1993. "A yearly mental training program for a college basketball player." *Sport Psychologist* 7:173–90.

Senqi, Hu, et al. 1992. "Positive thinking reduces heart rate and fear responses to speech-phobic imagery." *Perceptual and Motor Skills* 75:1067–73.

Sheikh, Anees A. 1989. *Healing from Within*. Milwaukee: American Imagery Institute, 34–40.

———, R. G. Kunzendorf. "Imagery, physiology, and psychosomatic illness." *International Review of Mental Imagery* 1:95–138.

Sheldrake, Rupert. 1981. *A New Science of Life: The Hypothesis of Formative Causation*. Los Angeles: Jeremy Tarcher.

———. 1988. *The Presence of the Past: Morphic Resonance and the Habits of Nature*. New York: Times Books.

Siegel, Bernard. 1986. *Love, Medicine and Miracles*. New York: Harper and Row.

Simonton, O. Carl, et al. 1978. *Getting Well Again.* New York: Bantam Books.

Sky, Michael. 1993. *Sexual Peace: Beyond the Dominator Virus.* Santa Fe: Bear Publishing Co.

Slomine, Beth, and Anthony Greene. 1993. "Anger imagery and corrugator electromyography." *Journal of Psychosomatic Research* 37:671–6.

Smith, Huston. 1991. *The World's Religions.* New York: HarperCollins.

Smith, John. 1992. *Women and Doctors.* New York: Atlantic Monthly Press.

Snyder, Solomon. 1980. "Brain peptides as neurotransmitters." *Science* 209 (August 29):976–83.

Sontag, Deborah. 1992. "Teachers' leader takes back old values." *New York Times* March 22.

Sperry, R. W. 1964. "The great cerebral commissure." *The Biological Bases of Behavior,* edited by J. McGaugh et al. San Francisco: W. H. Freeman.

———. 1968. "Hemispheric deconnection and unity in conscious awareness." *American Psychologist* 23 (10):723–33.

Steinfels, Peter. 1993. "An author causes a furor by saying science is a kind of faith that can't answer basic questions." *New York Times* March 20.

Stevens, William. 1992. "Talks seek to prevent huge loss of species." *New York Times* March 3.

Stevenson, Richard. 1992. "Challenge to London's lofty role." *New York Times* September 12.

Storer, John. 1956. *The Web of Life.* New York: New American Library.

———. 1968. *Man in the Web of Life.* New York: New American Library.

Suinn, Richard. 1983. "Imagery and sports." In *Imagery: Current Theory, Research and Application,* edited by A. Sheikh, pp. 507–534. New York: John Wiley and Sons.

Talbot, Michael. 1991. *The Holographic Universe.* New York: HarperCollins.

Toffler, Alvin. 1990. "Power shift." *Newsweek* October 15.

Tompkins, Peter, and Christopher Bird. 1973. *The Secret Life of Plants.* New York: Harper and Row.

Troesch, Lisa. 1994. "Mental relaxation cuts side effects." *USA Today* 123 (October): 7–8.

Vaughn, Frances. 1979. *Awakening Intuition.* Garden City: Doubleday.

von Franz, Marie Louise, and James Hillman. 1971. *Jung's Typology.* Dallas: Spring Publications.

von Oech, Roger. 1992. *Creative Whack Pack.* Stamford: U.S. Games Systems.

Weaver, Richard, and Howard Cotrell. 1991. "Guided mental imagery dynamation sequences as practical confrontation and intervention strategies for changing weak (non-constructive) business professionals' habits." *Bulletin of the Association for Business Communications* (September):91.

Wheatley, Margaret. 1992. *Leadership and the New Science.* San Francisco: Berrett-Koehler.

White, Lawrence Jr. 1992. "Don't handcuff the healthy banks." *New York Times* May 17.

Wilber, Ken. 1985. *The Holographic Paradigm and Other Paradoxes: Exploring the Leading Edge of Science.* Boston: Shambhala Publications.

———. 1985. *Quantum Questions: Mystical Writings of the World's Great Physicists.* Boston: Shambhala Publications.

Williams, Strephon. 1980. *Jungian-Senoi Dreamwork Manual.* Berkeley: Journey Press.

Wolf, Fred Alan. 1984. *Star Wave: Mind, Consciousness and Quantum Physics.* New York: Macmillan.

———. 1991. *The Eagle's Quest.* New York: Simon and Schuster.

Wriston, Walter. 1992a. "The decline of the central bankers." *New York Times* September 20.

———. 1992b. *The Twilight of Sovereignty.* New York: Charles Scribner's Sons.

Wynd, Christine. 1992. "Personal power imagery and relaxation techniques used in smoking cessation programs." *American Journal of Health Promotion* 6:184–9, 196.

Yogananda, Paramahansa. 1946. *Autobiography of a Yogi.* Los Angeles: Self-Realization Fellowship.

Authors' Request

Our research into the efficacy of intuitive imaging continues. We would appreciate hearing from readers who would be willing to share their experiences with the imaging process. While we are interested in all accounts, we are especially interested in examples of imaging applied in business. Please send stories of how imaging has been helpful, along with actual images and results, to us at the following address:

John Pehrson and Sue Mehrtens
5 Sombra del Monte
Placitas, NM 87043
email: jbpehrson@aol.com

Thank you.

Index

John B. Pehrson is president of Creative Change Technologies, a training and consulting firm dedicated to helping individuals and organizations live and work with a greater sense of purpose and potential. His efforts are focused on the areas of creativity, deep team building, and executive coaching.

A former executive with DuPont, Pehrson has more than twenty-three years of broad international business experience that includes business and technology management, strategic planning, product development, manufacturing, sales, and marketing.

John is the coauthor of two books: *Renewing Spirit and Learning in Business* and *Intuition at Work.* He lives in Placitas, New Mexico.

Dr. Susan E. Mehrtens is president of The Potlatch Group, a research organization specializing in analysis of business trends related to global evolution and social change. Her clients range from Fortune 500 companies like AT&T, DuPont, General Motors, and Sears to smaller businesses, schools, and private foundations, such as The Institute of Noetic Sciences and the World Business Academy.

After receiving her Ph.D. from Yale University, Mehrtens taught at Queens College, City University of New York, and the College of the Atlantic in Bar Harbor, Maine, in the fields of environmental studies, medieval studies, history, Latin, and Greek.

Sue is coauthor of *Earthkeeping,* an ecology text, and *The Fourth Wave,* a vision of business in the twenty-first century. She lives in Mineola, New York.

*For Product Safety Concerns and Information please contact
our EU representative GPSR@taylorandfrancis.com Taylor & Francis
Verlag GmbH, Kaufingerstraße 24, 80331 München, Germany*

T - #0079 - 230425 - C0 - 234/156/13 - PB - 9780750698054 - Gloss Lamination